12-15-12

Harriet Tubman

and the
Underground
Railroad

David A. Adler

Holiday House / New York

For Barbara and Elliot

Copyright © 2013 by David A. Adler
All rights reserved
HOLIDAY HOUSE is registered in the U.S. Patent and Trademark Office.
Printed and Bound in November 2012 at Worzalla, Stevens Point, WI, USA.
The text typeface is Oldbook ITC.
Illustration credits appear on page 136.
www.holidayhouse.com
First edition
1 3 5 7 9 10 8 6 4 2

Library of Congress Cataloging-in-Publication Data
Adler, David A.
Harriet Tubman and the underground railroad / by David A. Adler. — 1st ed.
p. cm.
Includes bibliographical references.
ISBN 978-0-8234-2365-1 (hardcover)
1. Tubman, Harriet, 1820?-1913—Juvenile literature. 2. Slaves—United States—
Biography—Juvenile literature. 3. African American women—Biography—Juvenile
literature. 4. Underground Railroad—Juvenile literature. I. Title.
E444.T82A59 2013
973.7'115092—dc23
[B]

Contents

Harriet Tubman (1823–1913)

PREFACE

In 1907, eighty-five-year-old Harriet Tubman was interviewed by a reporter for *The New York Herald*. At one point during their talk she looked beyond the reporter to a nearby apple orchard.

"Do you like apples?" she asked.

The reporter said he did.

"Did you ever plant any apple trees?"

"With shame," the reporter later wrote, "I confessed I had not."

"No," she said, "but somebody else planted them. I liked apples when I was young, and I said some day I'll plant apples myself for other young folks to eat, and I guess I done it."

Yes, she had.

Planting apples was her metaphor for a life spent in unselfish giving and doing for others. It was a life of courage, passion, and adventure.

Harriet Tubman was a hero to many of the most influential people of the nineteenth century, including Abraham Lincoln's secretary of state William Seward, the rabid abolitionist John Brown, women's-rights leader Susan B. Anthony, poet and essayist Ralph Waldo Emerson, and England's Queen Victoria.

She was greatly admired by Frederick Douglass, the world-renowned writer and speaker and a friend and adviser of President Lincoln.

"The midnight sky and the silent stars," Douglass wrote to her in 1868, "have been the witnesses of your devotion to freedom and to your heroism.... Much that you have done would seem improbable to those who do not know you as I know you. It is to me a great pleasure and a great privilege to bear testimony to your character and your works."

Chapter One

MINTY

The sad effects of slavery,
I can no longer stand;
I've served my master all my days,
without a dime reward.
—From the song Harriet Tubman sang
with Joe Bailey and the group of slaves
she led to freedom in 1856

JOSIAH "JOE" BAILEY was a tragic example of the horrors endured by millions of African Americans through much of the nineteenth century. He was a hard worker. For six years he had been hired out by his slaveholder to William Hughlett, a planter and lumber merchant on Maryland's Eastern Shore. One day in the fall of 1856, because he valued Bailey's work, Hughlett bought him, and early the next morning he woke him. "Now, Joe," he said, "strip and take a licking."

Bailey was puzzled. He did not understand why he was being punished.

"Haven't I always been faithful to you?" he asked. "Haven't I worked through sun and rain, early in the morning and late at night? . . . Have you anything to complain against me?"

"You belong to *me* now," Hughlett said. He was asserting

A slave about to be beaten

his power over his slave. The first lesson was to obey without question. "Now strip and take it."

Bailey knew that if he resisted he could be shot or hanged, so he took the beating, but he told himself, "This is the first and the last."

Late one night soon after his beating Bailey took a boat and rowed down the river to the Brodess plantation. There he told Old Ben Ross, "Next time Moses comes, let me know."

"Moses" was the nickname of Ross's daughter Harriet Tubman. Several years earlier she had escaped slavery. Then she risked her life and her freedom again and again to lead others out. Each trip was fraught with danger. Any runaway, including Tubman, who was caught, even in a free state, could be arrested, jailed, beaten, and even killed. "Keep going," Tubman told the runaways. "If you want to taste freedom, keep going." When one resisted she held a gun to his head and said, "Go on or die."

Tubman was the most famous "conductor" of the "Underground Railroad," the trail of safe houses for fugitive slaves on their way north. She proudly said of her many missions, "I never ran my train off track and I never lost a passenger."

During the Civil War, Tubman served the Union army as a laundress, cook, nurse, scout, and spy. After the war she fought for women's rights and set up a home for the poor and elderly. She was a courageous, selfless woman devoted to helping others.

෨෧

Harriet Tubman was born a slave in Dorchester County on the Eastern Shore of Maryland. Many historians believe she was born in 1822. But like many slaves, she was never sure of the exact day or year of her birth. "I never met a slave," Frederick Douglass once wrote, "who could tell me with any certainty how old he was.... Masters allowed no questions to be put to them by slaves concerning their ages. Such questions were regarded by the masters as evidence of an impudent curiosity."

Tubman's parents were Harriet "Rit" Green and Benjamin "Old Ben" Ross. They had perhaps as many as eleven children. Harriet was somewhere in the middle. Her parents named her Araminta and called her "Minty." In her early twenties, when she married John Tubman, she became Minty Tubman. Soon after that she took her mother's first name and was known as Harriet Tubman.

Minty's parents were slaves of Edward and Eliza Brodess, poor farmers, and of Edward's stepfather, Anthony Thompson. Thompson grew wheat, rye, corn, and apples on his farm, and also owned acres of wooded land.

Minty's father worked in the woods cutting down trees, hauling and shipping the lumber to Baltimore Harbor where it was used to build boats. In his spare time he made household items from wood. He carved the wooden cradle Minty slept in as an infant.

Minty's mother, Harriet Green, was a house slave and worked from early morning until well after nightfall.

Beyond the great injustice of working without pay and at the whim of their slaveholders, Ben Ross and Harriet Green were never sure where they or their children would be from week to week or month to month. Since the Brodesses had lots of expenses and little luck farming, they often sent their slaves to work for others. Whatever the slaves earned was paid to the Brodesses. Slaves could even be sold and sent far away from their families, with little hope of ever returning.

Slave trading was big business then, partly because of laws meant to restrict slavery. Beginning in 1808, it was a crime to bring slaves into the country. This meant the only legal way to get a mature slave was to buy him from someone else. Throughout the first half of the nineteenth century even free blacks weren't safe. Slave traders sometimes kidnapped and sold them.

In the 1830s Edward Brodess sold two of Minty's sisters. One sister left behind two young children. Some time after that a trader from Georgia visited Brodess. They talked for a while. Then Brodess called for Minty's brother Moses to come

Slaves being sold at auction

to the house. Rit Green knew about the trader. She suspected she was about to lose another child and was determined not to let that happen.

Rit Green went to the house instead of Moses. "What do you want of the boy?" she asked.

Brodess didn't answer.

A slave cabin

Green went back to her work and Brodess called again for Moses. This time he said he needed him to hitch the trader's horse to his carriage.

Again, Green went to the house.

Brodess was angry. He hadn't called for Green. "I hollered for the boy," he said.

Green cursed and said she knew he wanted Moses for that "Georgia man" and she wouldn't let that happen. She hid her son first in a nearby forest and then in friends' houses.

Brodess was desperate for cash and determined to make the sale. He kept the trader's money and told him to come back when he was done with all his other business.

Soon after that Brodess came to Rit Green's cabin.

"The first man that comes into my house," Green hollered, "I will split his head open."

Brodess knew Rit Green and knew this was no idle threat. He backed off. Green kept Moses hidden until the trader was on his way back to Georgia.

There was a lot of Rit Green's feistiness and strong will in Minty Ross. This one time Rit Green had saved her son from being sold, but she and her family were still slaves. It was Minty who years later led Moses and most of her other family members to freedom.

Slave children

Chapter Two

HAIR SAVES
HER LIFE

I grew up like a neglected weed.
—Harriet Tubman

THE CHILDHOOD OF a slave was short. At the age of about five Minty was given her first job. She was left to take care of her younger brother Ben. Young Minty was playful and made a game of baby-sitting. One of her games was "pig in a bag." She held Ben upside down by his baggy clothing and swung him around.

At six, Minty was sent to work for James Cook and his wife, poor white farmers who lived a few miles away at the edge of a swamp. Minty thought of this as some great adventure. When Cook came for her, she was anxious to go. They traveled by horseback, arriving at the farm when the Cooks' two children were eating dinner. Mrs. Cook offered Minty a glass of milk but she wouldn't take it. "I never ate in the house where the white people was," Tubman said later, "and I was ashamed to stand up and eat before them."

After supper Minty was left alone in the kitchen where she was expected to sleep. By then she was ready to go home.

"If I could only get home and get in my mother's bed," she thought, and cried herself to sleep. "The funny part of that," she said later, was that her mother "never had a bed in her life. Nothing but a board box nailed up against the wall and straw laid on it."

Mrs. Cook tried to teach her young slave to weave cloth, but Minty was either a poor student or too stubborn to obey her mistress. At last Mrs. Cook gave up. Minty's next job was to wade barefoot into the swamp and check on the Cooks' muskrat traps, an unpleasant job, especially in cold weather, which was unfortunately the best time to catch the animals. The Cooks sent Minty to see to the traps even when she had the measles. As a result she got so sick she had to be sent home, where her mother cared for her.

When Minty recovered she was sent back. Mrs. Cook tried again to teach her to weave, but the strong-willed Minty refused to learn.

After two frustrating years with the Cooks, Minty was sent back to Brodess.

She was happy to be home again, but she was not there for long. She was soon hired out to someone she remembered only as "Miss Susan." It was Minty's job to take care of Miss Susan's baby, to keep it quiet. If the child cried, Minty was beaten. When the baby slept, Minty was to do household chores, such as sweep and dust, and if she didn't do a proper job of it, she was severely punished. She later remembered that she was once whipped five times before breakfast.

At night it was Minty's job to rock the baby's cradle. If after her long day at work she dozed a bit and the child cried, down would come the whip. Perhaps this is when Minty learned to stay awake even when she was exhausted, a skill that helped her years later when she needed to be alert through the night to hide from slave catchers.

One day Miss Susan "got into a great quarrel with her husband; she had an awful temper," Tubman remembered many years later. Miss Susan's back was turned and there was some sugar nearby. "Now, you know I never had anything good...so I put my fingers in the sugar bowl to take one lump and maybe she heard me, for she turned and saw me. The next minute she had the rawhide down." This time Minty decided she wasn't going to be hit. She ran off.

Minty knew that if any of her mistress's neighbors found her they would send her back, so she ran a long way. She ran until she was so tired that she fell into a pigpen with an old sow and eight or ten piglets. "I was so beat out I couldn't stir." She stayed somehow hidden in the pigs' slop. She fought the pigs for potato peels and other scraps. "The old sow would push me away when I tried to get her children's food, and I was awful afraid of her."

Minty landed in the pigpen on a Friday, and by the following Tuesday was so hungry that she knew she had to go back. But she also knew what was coming. When she returned, Miss Susan's husband gave her an awful whipping.

With little to eat and constant beatings, Minty was soon emaciated and scarred. Miss Susan no longer wanted the skinny, uncooperative slave, so she sent her back to Brodess.

Again, Minty wasn't home for long. She was soon hired by someone she described as "close to the worst man in the neighborhood." He sent her out to harvest flax. The fibers inside flax plants were used to make rope as well as woven into a rough fabric often used to make slaves' clothes. Each plant had to be pulled from the ground, roots and all. It was hard work, but Minty didn't mind. She preferred to be outside rather than under the constant watch of a mistress.

She often ate her midday meal in the field, without the niceties of plates and napkins. Any scraps of meat she was given were fatty and probably cooked in lard.

Minty said later that as she worked, "My hair had never been combed and it stood out like a bushel basket. When I got through eating I'd wipe the grease off my fingers on my hair," probably to hold it down.

One day the cook asked Minty to come with her to the village store. Minty wrapped a shawl over her unruly hair and went along. The cook walked into the store and Minty stood by the doorway.

Inside, a slave and his overseer were arguing. The slave ran toward the door and the overseer called for Minty to stop him. She refused. The overseer took a two-pound lead weight from the counter and threw it. He hoped to hit his slave, but he hit Minty instead.

"That was the last I knew," she said later. "That weight struck me in the head and broke my skull and cut a piece of that shawl clean off and drove it into my head. They carried me to the house all bleeding and fainting. I had no bed, no place to lie down on at all, and they lay me on the seat of the loom, and I stayed there all that day and the next, and the next day I went to work again and there I worked with the blood and sweat rolling down my face till I couldn't see."

Her hair mixed with grease had cushioned the blow. It may have saved her life, but still, the injury left its mark, a permanent dent in her forehead. It also caused episodes of narcolepsy, a medical condition that made her suddenly fall asleep, which plagued her the rest of her life. Sometimes she dozed off in the middle of a conversation. A few minutes later she would wake up, not even aware that she had been sleeping, and just continue talking.

It was after her injury that Minty began having visions of flying over fields and rivers, of looking down on them "like a bird." She heard voices and saw bright, colorful lights that no one else heard or saw.

In one of her first visions, Minty describes that "we'd been carting manure all day. The other girl and I were going home on the side of the cart, and another boy was driving, when suddenly I heard such music as filled all the air." She saw a vision similar to those described in the Bible. When her master tried to wake her, Minty told him that she hadn't been asleep.

She also had visions of horsemen and heard the screams of frightened women and children, surely as they were about to be sold and taken from their families. "I seemed to see a line," she said later. She was on one side. On the other "were green fields, and lovely flowers, and beautiful white ladies, who stretched out their arms to me over the line, but I couldn't reach them." In her visions Minty could never get to the other side.

THE LIBERATOR.

DECEMBER 16, 183[?]

SLAVE CHILDREN'S PRAYER, Boston, Massachusetts, the Sabbath School Instructor.

Hear our prayer, most holy Father! While we raise our voice to thee; —Africa's children thou canst gather In thy arms, and make them free. Come, we pray thee, near, and bless us—We are weak and helpless now—For thy *servants*, Lord, distress us, When we would before thee bow. Break our chains, while we are calling Humbly on thy holy name; May the lash to earth be falling, Not upon a human frame. May the white man see his error.... Hear, and kindly bless to-day.

Excerpted from

THE NORTH STAR
APRIL 7, 1849

SLAVERY IN THE DISTRICT OF COLUMBIA: REVOLTING PICTURE. —I turned to look for the doomed. She stood upon the auction stand. In stature she was of the middle size, slim and delicately built... Now despair sat on her countenance. O! I shall never forget that look...

'How much is said for this beautiful and healthy *slave girl*...—Who bids?' 'Five hundred dollars,' 'Eight hundred,' 'One thousand,' were soon bid by different purchasers...'She is intelligent, well informed, easy to communicate, a first rate instructress.' This had the desired effect. 'Twelve hundred,' 'Fourteen,' 'Sixteen,' quickly followed. He read again—'She is a devoted Christian, sustains the best of morals, and is perfectly trusty.' This raised the bids to two thousand dollars, at which she was struck off. —Here closed one of the darkest scenes in the book of time. This was an auction at which the bones, muscles, sinews, blood and nerves of a young lady of nineteen sold for one thousand dollars; her improved intellect for six hundred more...

Excerpted from
The National Era
JULY 29, 1847

ANOTHER CASE. —We published lately, from the *Charleston Courier,* the report of proceedings in the case of a white woman tried for the murder of her slave. It was proved, it will be recollected, that the slave girl died under correction administered by the command of her mistress; but the latter was acquitted, on her own oath, that being sufficient according to the law, to clear her, unless opposed by the testimony of two white witnesses…On the night of the 4th of July, the weather being very inclement, sudden indisposition in a member of the family aroused Mr. Toomer between 12 and 1 o'clock. Finding that the servant who usually slept in the house was not in, "he proceeded to the yard, where he saw an upper room of his kitchen lighted up; on entering and making his presence known, the lights were instantly extinguished and the door bolted. By the assistance of some of his other servants, being prevented from escaping, he arrested thirteen negroes, including six of his own. They were engaged in supping with his own furniture and property in use. The undersigned caused his slave Carolina to inflict upon each, except Mary, the slave of Mr. Carew, fifty lashes with a cowskin. On Mary, Carolina, by the direction of the undersigned, inflicted *ten* lashes; this was in consideration of her having a young infant with her at the time; she was then dismissed… Mr. Toomer informed deponent he had flogged Mary to his satisfaction…From the exposure, whipping, and fright, irritation and fever followed, immediately developing inflammation on the breasts, and the result was *death*…Mr. Toomer evidently entertains no doubt that the statement he makes will completely exculpate him in the judgment of his fellow-citizens. He expresses no regret at the result of his "terrible discipline;" seems not to imagine that he has done any act out of the usual order of things.

Reports in African-American newspapers, reflect the conditions of slavery during the period

Free states and slave states

Chapter Three

TALKING TO THE LORD

Every time I saw a white man
I was afraid of being carried away.
—Harriet Tubman in an 1855 interview

HOW COULD SO many people in the pro-slavery South justify their actions, the cruelty to their slaves? The story they told was that the slave population was "a happy one," according to one Virginia legislator, "a contented, peaceful, and harmless one." It wasn't. There were many relatively quiet protests—slacking off, pretending to be sick or injured. There was also arson and outright rebellions.

In 1800 Gabriel Prosser led about fifty armed slaves on an unsuccessful march on Richmond, Virginia. First a storm stopped the uprising. Then state militia arrested Prosser and twenty-five others.

In 1811 Charles Deslondes led a few hundred slaves on a march in New Orleans, Louisiana. Eighty-two of them were killed. The heads of sixteen were stuck on the ends of wooden poles and displayed as a warning to others. The most dire punishment was saved for Deslondes. His hands were chopped off. He was shot in both legs and in his chest, and set on fire.

In 1822 Denmark Vesey, an African-American ship's carpenter who had bought his freedom, plotted a rebellion in Charleston, South Carolina. For months he and his lieutenants worked on plans to capture weapons and guardhouses. Any whites they met were to be killed. At the last moment someone betrayed Vesey, and more than 130 blacks were arrested. Thirty-seven of them were executed, including Denmark Vesey.

In 1831 the most famous of all the slave revolts broke out under the leadership of Nat Turner, a slave and Baptist preacher. He began with just twenty to thirty others. By the second day thirty to fifty more had joined the uprising. They brutally killed about fifty whites in Southampton County, Virginia. A huge force of armed whites gathered and fought back. About one hundred blacks were killed. Their leader, Nat Turner, was captured and hanged.

The Turner revolt led to widespread panic throughout the South.

The capture of Nat Turner

There were approximately two million slaves in the United States. What if they all rebelled?

Restrictions on slaves and free African Americans became even more stringent. Laws were enacted forbidding African Americans from gathering without the supervision of whites. In some states, blacks were not allowed to own drums, whistles, or other musical instruments. In Louisiana anyone convicted of teaching or in any way enabling a black to read and write could be sentenced to one year in jail. A Mississippi law forbade free blacks from living in the state.

Harriet Tubman's home state of Maryland seemed especially susceptible to rebellion. More than one-third of its population was African American, and more than one-third of them were free and considered to be potential troublemakers. Suspicions were so widespread that in 1832 some state lawmakers proposed that free blacks be forced to leave and kept from returning to Maryland. The proposition didn't get enough support to become law.

For some Maryland slaveholders the easy answer to possible revolt was to free their slaves. Others sold them to traders who locked them in chain gangs and took them to the Deep South. Two of Minty's sisters had already been taken off. She was afraid that one day she and the rest of her family would be sold, too.

She had good reason to worry. Her owner lived on land that barely produced a profit. Minty knew Brodess might pay his mounting debt by selling his most valuable assets, his slaves.

After Minty recovered from her head injury she was sent to work for neighbors as a field hand, plowing, planting, driving ox teams, and lifting heavy barrels. Soon she was as strong as any of the men. Looking back, she said, "Appears like I was

Slaves working in a cotton field in Georgia

getting fitted for the word the Lord was getting ready for me," the word to lead her brethren to freedom.

At about fourteen Minty worked for John Stewart, the owner of a shipyard, windmill, blacksmith shops, and corn and wheat fields. He found Minty to be a reliable worker, high-spirited, smart, and strong. She worked for Stewart for the next five to six years.

At first she worked as his house slave, cleaning, making beds, and beating the feather quilts. When the quilts were loose and comfortable she often jumped onto them and rested, a short break in her work-filled day.

Minty had no schooling, but according to the Reverend

E.U.A. Brooks of Utica, New York, who knew her, "She was very alert and possessed a splendid memory." With one of her masters, likely Stewart, her job was to accompany children to and from school. In the afternoon, if she arrived early to pick them up, she waited. According to a story told about her, one day she heard the teacher ask if anyone could spell the word "baker." When no one responded, Minty stood by the school door and called out "B-A-K-E-R."

Minty and her father cut down trees and chopped logs for Stewart. They worked in logging camps and loaded lumber onto ships with many free blacks. Surely this is how Minty first learned about the Underground Railroad, the many people willing to open their homes to runaway slaves. Perhaps she heard from her free coworkers about abolitionists, people in free states who were fighting slavery.

One of the free African Americans she met was John Tubman. He was about ten years older and ten inches taller than Minty. There is no record of their courtship, but in 1844 they married. Minty Ross was now Minty Tubman, and would soon be called Harriet Tubman.

In 1847 she had her first small taste of freedom. She arranged to pay Brodess a yearly fee of fifty to sixty dollars. Then she hired herself to others, and whatever she earned over the yearly fee was hers to keep. Perhaps her hope was that she would earn enough extra money to one day buy her freedom. That never happened, but she did earn enough to buy two steers. Now when someone hired her he got the animals working for him, too. With the steers to help her, Tubman could demand more money for a day's work.

Tubman also paid a lawyer to look into the legal records of Atthow Pattison, her mother's first owner. Pattison had died in 1797, and the lawyer found that according to the terms of his will his female slaves were to be set free when they reached the age of forty-five. Rit Green was already past sixty and should have been a free woman. The lawyer also told Tubman that slaves whose time of service was limited were not to be sold out of Maryland, so the sale of Rit Green's daughters to the Deep South had been illegal. It was a cruel irony that Green, who legally should have been free, could not take her case to court because she was *not* free. Slaves couldn't bring any legal actions.

Tubman was outraged. But she wasn't naive. Brodess was still desperate for money. Despite the law she knew that one day she could be sold off.

"Every time I saw a white man," she said later, "I was afraid I was being carried away."

One time her poor health saved her.

She had been sick and bedridden from December 1848 until March 1849. During that time Brodess tried to sell her, but no one would buy a sickly slave.

When she recovered, she heard a rumor that she and her brother would soon be sold and sent to the Deep South to work in the cotton and rice fields.

In the past she had prayed for Brodess: "O dear Lord, change that man's heart and make him a Christian." On March 1, 1849, she prayed, "If you ain't never going to change that man's heart, *kill him*, Lord, and take him out of the way, so he won't do no more mischief."

Less that one week later, on March 7, Brodess was dead. "He died just as he had lived," Tubman said later, "a bad, wicked man."

He was just forty-seven years old.

Tubman felt her prayer had caused her master's death. "I'd give all the world full of gold, if I had it, to bring that poor soul back," she said later. "But I couldn't pray for him no longer."

Her prayer, though she regretted it, had been answered. From then on she felt she had a special closeness with God.

"I was always talking to the Lord.... When I went to the horse-trough to wash my face, and took the water in my hands, I said, 'O Lord, wash me, make me clean... wipe away all my sins.'"

With Brodess dead, what would happen to his slaves?

Brodess's death did not bring her any comfort. Tubman began to have nightmares of being taken off in a chain gang. In the middle of the night she woke up and cried out, "They're coming, they're coming. I must go." Her husband laughed and called her a fool. With her master dead, he said, the danger was gone.

John Tubman was wrong.

Brodess's widow, Eliza, was left with several young children and lots of debt. She had to borrow from a neighbor to pay bills. In June, just three months after the death of her husband, Eliza Brodess tried to auction off Harriet's sister, niece, and her niece's two-year-old daughter, but various legal complications stopped the sales. Eliza Brodess hired a lawyer to appeal the court's ruling.

Harriet felt it was time for her and her family to run.

She told her brothers Robert, Ben, and Henry they must leave that Saturday night. Because Sunday was a day off, they wouldn't be missed until Monday. By that time they should be far away.

Tubman and her brothers ran off. They probably went alongside one of the many creeks on the Eastern Shore of Maryland. They didn't know where they were going, just that they were headed north toward the free states of Pennsylvania and New Jersey. They knew that if they were

Slaves escaping from the eastern shore of Maryland

caught, they would be severely beaten and perhaps even be sold to slaveholders in the Deep South, where escape would be much more difficult.

It was dark. Tubman and her brothers heard the night calls of owls and wild animals. Her brothers were frightened, and they all went back.

Then Harriet heard that what she feared most was about to happen. She was about to be sold. This time she decided to run off alone.

"Go along," she told her mother, who was on her way to milk the cows. "I'll do the milking tonight." She put on her sunbonnet, did the milking, and went to the "big house." She delivered the milk and went outside and sang what sounded like a hymn. She sang of Moses, who more than three thousand years before had led the Israelites from slavery to freedom. She sang of the chariot that would take them to the promised land.

> *When that old chariot comes*
> *I'm going to leave you,*
> *I'm bound for the promised land.*
> *Friends, I'm going to leave you.*

Harriet Tubman knew that at first her family and friends might not understand her message, but once she was gone, they would.

> *I'm sorry, friends, to leave you,*
> *Farewell! Oh, farewell!*
> *But I'll meet you in the morning,*
> *Farewell! Oh, farewell!*
> *I'll meet you in the morning,*
> *When you reach the promised land;*
> *On the other side of Jordan,*
> *For I'm bound for the promised land.*

That night Harriet Tubman searched the sky for the North Star, and with that as her guide she started out.

She was determined.

She was fearless.

"I had reasoned this out in my mind," she said later. "There was two things I had a *right* to, liberty or death; if I could not have one, I would have the other, for no man should take me alive; I should fight for my liberty as long as my strength lasted, and when the time came for me to go, the Lord would let them take me."

Chapter Four

A GLORY OVER EVERYTHING

I felt like I was in heaven.
—Harriet Tubman, remembering
her first taste of freedom

ON SEPTEMBER 17, 1849, Harriet Tubman ran to the home of a white Quaker woman, probably Hannah Leverton, who lived nearby and was known to help escaped slaves. Tubman came with a gift, a prized bed quilt she had made from scraps of cloth. Leverton told her where to go next, to the house of someone farther north, another "station" of the Underground Railroad. She also gave Tubman a paper with two names on it and told her to give the paper to the woman at the next house.

Tubman was on her first journey on the Railroad, a passenger on her way to freedom.

When she arrived at the second house, the woman there gave her a broom and told her to sweep the yard. That was to fool anyone passing by, who would surely assume Tubman worked there and would not suspect she was a fugitive slave.

When the woman's husband came home he hid Tubman in the back of his wagon, covered her with a cloth, and drove off. He stopped and left her outside of town with directions to another stop on the Railroad.

Historians trace the beginning of the Underground Railroad to 1804 when the white people of Columbia, Pennsylvania, helped a group of runaway slaves. The practice spread among some Quakers and in time to other religious groups including Dunkers, Wesleyan Methodists, Jews, Unitarians, Covenanters, and Roman Catholics. It spread from Pennsylvania to New Jersey and New York. In 1815 the Underground Railroad "track" was laid in Ohio. Soon there were safe houses as far away as Maine, Iowa, and Canada. Many of the people willing to open their homes to fugitive slaves were free blacks or former slaves who had themselves run away.

It's believed the Railroad got its name in 1831 when a slave named Tice Davis of Kentucky ran off. He swam across the

A slave escaping on the top of a train

Ohio River with his master chasing after him in a small boat. His master lost sight of Davis and couldn't find him when he came ashore. In frustration he said Davis "must have gone off on an underground road." In the 1830s there was great excitement about the new steam-powered trains and the expansion of railroad lines. As slaves continued to disappear the underground network that helped them became known as the Underground Railroad.

Tubman knew to follow the North Star toward the free states. On cloudy nights when the star was not visible she looked for moss which grows on the north sides of trees where there was less sunlight. After many days she had gone through Maryland and Delaware and into the free states of New Jersey and Pennsylvania. She said later that when she crossed from slavery to freedom, "I looked at my hands to see if I was the same person....There was such a glory over everything, the sun came like gold through the trees, and over the fields, and I felt like I was in heaven."

There was some irony in her freedom. When she was a slave, her greatest fear was that she would be sold and separated from her family. Now with her escape she had done that to herself. She was free, but she was alone.

Slaves escaping by boat

Tubman thought of a man she knew who had been in prison for twenty-five years. "He was always thinking of his home, and counting by years, months, and days the time till he should be free, and see his family and friends once more." When at last he was free and went home to the house he had lived in as child, he found it was no longer there. His family was gone. No one in his old town even remembered them. "There was no one to take him by the hand to welcome him back to life."

That's how Harriet Tubman felt.

"I had crossed the line of which I had so long been dreaming. I was free, but there was no one to welcome me to the land of freedom."

Back in Dorchester County, surely Eliza Brodess knew Tubman had run off, but she waited five weeks, until the end of October, to post a reward for her capture. The advertisement appeared in *The Delaware Gazette* and *The Cambridge Chronicle* and listed three slaves as runaways, Harriet and her brothers Ben and Henry, who was listed as Harry in the ad. "MINTY," it said, "aged about twenty-seven, is of chestnut color, fine looking, and about 5 feet high. One hundred dollars reward for each of the above named negroes, if taken out of the State, and $50 each if taken in the State."

Why were her brothers listed in the advertisement? Why did Brodess wait so long to run it?

The information on Tubman's first attempt with her brothers and on her successful escape comes from interviews with her many years later. Perhaps by then either she didn't remember exactly what happened, or people were careless when they recorded her words.

It could be that when Harriet Tubman first ran away she and her brothers wandered for a few weeks. It's also possible that after she ran off alone her brothers went looking for her, so they were missing, too.

Tubman made her way to Philadelphia, Pennsylvania, a haven for free African Americans. There were more than twenty public

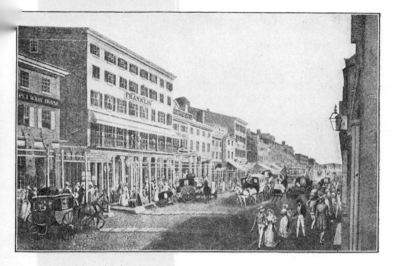

*Philadelphia,
around 1800*

and private schools for blacks in Philadelphia at that time. The city had a far higher number of free blacks in school than any other city in the country. Many blacks owned property there. They worked as servants, coachmen, laborers, craftsmen, barbers, washerwomen, seamstresses, and cooks. Lawmakers in Pennsylvania had made the state a good place for runaways. Just two years earlier they had passed a "personal liberty" law that made it illegal for slaveholders to travel with slaves through the state, or to hold fugitive slaves in state jails.

Over the next year Tubman worked as a servant and cook in private homes and hotels. In the summer she was employed in Cape May, New Jersey, a seaside resort. During this time she stayed connected with her family through a network of free blacks, runaways, and anti-slavery activists.

She worked hard, saved as much money as she could, and made plans to rescue her family.

"I was free and they should be free," she decided. "I would make a home for them in the North, and the Lord helping me, I would bring them all there." She prayed, "O dear Lord...come to my help."

With her escape, she had been a passenger on the Railroad. Soon she would become its most famous conductor. She would make many risky trips back to Maryland and rescue her family, friends, and others.

Ellen Craft and her husband, William Craft, slaves in Macon, Georgia, used especially creative disguises.

Ellen Craft was fair-skinned. She dressed as a man. She had her hair cut short, and to hide that she had no beard, she pretended to have a toothache and wrapped her face in bandages. She wore eyeglasses and pretended to be deaf. She limped and carried a cane in her left hand, and, probably because she was never taught to read and write and was therefore unable to sign her name, she put her right arm in a sling. Her husband, William, pretended to be her servant. They traveled safely in their disguises through four slave states, South Carolina and North Carolina, Virginia, and Maryland, and settled in the free state of Massachusetts.

William Craft

Ellen Craft

Report from
FREDERICK DOUGLASS' PAPER
An African-American Newspaper
FEBRUARY 9, 1855

RUNAWAY SLAVES
THE ***UNDERGROUND RAIL-ROAD.*** The travel over the ***underground railroad*** for the past few days has been, we are informed, unusually active, and no fewer than seven lots of runaway slaves have arrived at this terminus within a week. The first of these lots was composed of three men; the next of three; the third, of two men; the fifth of one man. All these were from Kentucky. The sixth lot was composed of two middle-aged, stout men, who had come on foot from Louisiana to this place, sleeping by day, and walking toward the North Star at night. They arrived here on Wednesday, and after recruiting, are to be sent over the ***Underground Railroad*** to Canada.

The last lot was composed of a mother and three children, who came upon the mail boat from Louisville, and were to be taken to Paris, Kentucky. She managed to get to some Abolitionists, and was immediately sent north. The total loss to the master, from the escape of these fifteen slaves, must exceed fifteen thousand dollars. A colored woman named Johanna Piles is now in Cincinnati, soliciting funds to purchase her husband, who is a slave in Washington County, Kentucky. The wife and two children, with sixteen others, were manumitted about a year since by their mistress, who then resided in Washington County, Kentucky, but located these she set free in Iowa.

Cincinnati Columbian, Jan. 29

Chapter Five

THE UNDERGROUND RAILROAD

Joe, you're in Queen Victoria's dominions.
You're a free man.
—Harriet Tubman in 1856, on entering
Canada with Joe Bailey and several
other runaways

SLAVES ESCAPED FROM bondage in cities and on plantations, from kitchens and cotton fields. They came mostly from border states, but also from states in the Deep South. Many ran from cruel masters, but some slaves, because they longed to be free, left even good masters. They usually ran off with almost nothing, not even food or money. Many left without a planned route of escape, with just the North Star to guide them. They were chased by gun-toting slave hunters with bloodhounds. Runaways were lucky if they somehow found someone willing to hide them on their way north. They were especially fortunate if they had someone to lead them from one safe home to the next along the Underground Railroad—someone like Harriet Tubman.

There were codes and passwords on the Railroad, on what it called its "grapevine telegraph." Late at night there would be a few light knocks at a window. Someone inside would whisper "Who's there?" At many houses—"stations"—the accepted answer was "A friend with friends." In York, Pennsylvania, the password was "William Penn."

There were coded notes sent ahead so "stationmasters" would be ready to help fugitives coming their way. Among the many messages found after the Civil War were "By tomorrow evening's mail, you will receive two volumes of the 'Irrepressible Conflict' bound in black. After perusal, please forward and advise" and "Look for those fleeces of wool by tomorrow. Send them to test the market and price, no back charges."

Harriet Tubman and the many other fearless people who helped runaways were called "stationmasters," "conductors," "agents," and "brakemen." The people they helped were called "parcels." The trains were sometimes farm wag-

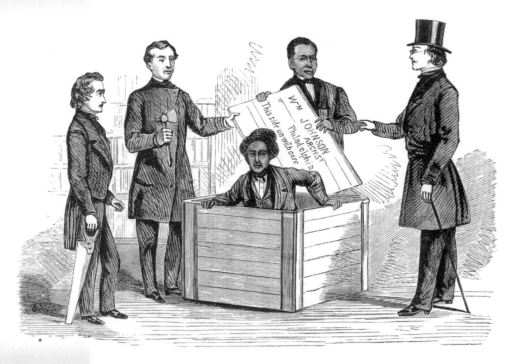

Henry "Box" Brown on his arrival in Philadelphia

ons with flat beds, and fugitives were hidden on them beneath cloths and produce as they were moved from one station to the next. Runaway slaves also traveled in rowboats and on foot. The safe houses where runaways could get food, shelter, and advice were called "stations" and "depots." The people who contributed money and clothing for the fugitives were called "Railroad stockholders."

John Greenleaf Whittier

Levi Coffin is credited with personally helping more than three thousand slaves escape, and was sometimes referred to as the president of the Railroad. He owned a "free labor goods" store in Cincinnati, Ohio. Nothing he sold was made or grown with slave labor.

According to one newspaper report the Railroad was "the most successful secret organization that ever existed in this country." In an 1898 study Professor Wilbur Siebert named some 3200 agents of the Railroad. Every one of those agents was a hero who risked his or her life to protest the injustice of slavery.

How successful was it?

Some studies estimate the number of its passengers at more than one hundred thousand. Even the many slaves who never fled may have benefited from the Railroad. Stories of it made slaveholders uneasy about holding on to what they considered their "property." Sometimes this led to better treatment of their slaves so they would be less tempted to run.

Among the many stationmasters were the former runaway slave Frederick Douglass, the poet and philosopher Henry David Thoreau of Massachusetts, the great poet John Greenleaf Whittier, and women's-rights advocates Susan B. Anthony, Angelina and Sarah Grimke, Lydia Maria Child, Abby Kelly, and Lucretia Mott.

Susan B. Anthony

Lucritia Mott

Lucretia Mott founded the Philadelphia Female Anti-Slavery Society in 1833. "If our principles are right," she said, "why should we be cowards?" Mott gave Harriet Tubman financial support and introduced her to local leaders of the abolitionist movement.

Agents often provided the runaways with elaborate disguises, including wigs and fake beards and moustaches. They dressed men as women and women as men. They also gave runaways farm tools to carry so it would look as if they were on their way to work.

Among Tubman's disguises were silk dresses, too elegant for any slave. One of her favorite props was a newspaper. Since slaveholders did not teach their slaves to read, any African American with a newspaper in the 1850s was often presumed to be a free black. This ploy fooled A. C. Thompson, someone Tubman was hired out to while she was a slave. While she was a fugitive, Thompson saw her pretending to read and walked right by her.

Even her singing saved her.

Once while she was riding on a stagecoach she was questioned by some men who suspected she might be a runaway. "Gentlemen," she said, "let me sing for you." And she sang until the next station, where she quickly got off the stagecoach.

Another time, in Dorchester County, Maryland, Tubman wore a large bonnet pulled down over her face. She carried two live chickens and walked bent, like an elderly woman. When she saw someone who knew her, she poked the chickens. They flapped their wings and made such a loud fuss that the acquaintance just hurried past.

Runaways were often forced to hide.

One time Tubman and the six slaves with her hid in holes dug to plant potatoes. Then they covered themselves with dirt.

Some stationmasters created unique hiding places for their passengers. At a station in Plainfield, Illinois, there was a secret room hidden inside a woodpile. The Reverend J. Porter of Green Bay, Wisconsin, hid runaways in his church's belfry. Bull's Tavern, run by Edward Morris in Pennsdale, Pennsylvania, was nicknamed "The House of Many Stairs" for its seven staircases. Runaways being chased by slave catchers were led down the maze of stairs to a secret room. The Reverend John Rankin of Ripley, Ohio, had a secret cellar in his barn. His house was on a hill overlooking the Ohio River, just across from the slave state of Kentucky. He left a burning lantern atop a flagpole so runaways could find him.

Not all runaways went north. Some in the Deep South ran to Mexico, which had abolished slavery in 1829. Others escaped to Florida and hid in the Everglades with American Indians.

Some agents made great sacrifices for the Railroad.

Thomas Garrett of Delaware paid huge fines and once told the judge, "Thee hasn't left me a dollar, but I wish to say to thee...if anyone knows of a fugitive who wants shelter, and a friend, *send him to Thomas Garrett.*" At one time it was reported that a ten-thousand-dollar reward was offered for his capture. Garrett wrote to a local newspaper that he was worth at least twenty thousand dollars, and if that much was offered he would surrender and collect the reward himself. Garrett was once asked how Harriet Tubman had the courage to make so many trips south. He answered that she had "confidence in the voice of God," whom she felt spoke "directly to her soul."

William Still, the son of slaves, was a stationmaster of the Underground Railroad and the corresponding secretary and later chairman of the Vigilance Committee of the Pennsylvania Anti-Slavery Society. He kept careful records of the many runaways who passed through Philadelphia. He interviewed the fugitives and recorded their stories. He hid the papers until after the Civil War and then published them.

In December 1854 he recorded the arrival of six passengers with their "Moses," Harriet Tubman. Still wrote, "She had faithfully gone down into Egypt, and had delivered these six bondmen by her own heroism. Harriet was a woman of no pretensions, indeed, a more ordinary specimen of humanity could hardly be found among the most unfortunate-looking farmhands of the South. Yet, in point of courage, shrewdness, and disinterested exertions to rescue her fellow-men, by making personal visits to Maryland among the slaves, she was without equal."

William Still

Still wrote, "Her success was wonderful. Time and again she made successful visits to Maryland on the Underground Rail Road, and would be absent for weeks, at a time, running daily risks while making preparations for herself and passengers. Great fears were entertained for her safety, but she seemed wholly devoid of personal fear. The idea of being captured by slave-hunters or slave-holders, seemed never to enter her mind....Half the time, she had the appearance of one asleep, and would actually sit down by the road-side and go fast asleep when on her errands of mercy through the South, yet, she would not suffer one of her party to whimper once, about 'giving out and going back,' however wearied they might be from hard travel day and night....Of course Harriet was supreme, and her followers generally

had full faith in her, and would back up any word she might utter.... Her like probably was never known before or since."

"Moses has got the charm," one of the slaves she rescued said. "The whites can't catch Moses because she's born with the charm. The Lord has given Moses the power."

Harriet Tubman agreed. She felt that God protected her.

She told a woman from Boston who was active in the anti-slavery cause about the time she waited in the woods to meet with some runaways to guide them to freedom. It was a stormy, snowy night and the fugitives never came. "Didn't you almost feel when you were lying alone, as if there were no God?" the woman from Boston asked. "Oh, no!" Tubman answered. "I just asked Jesus to take care of me, and He never let me get frostbitten one bit."

Tubman was often asked how she could risk her life and freedom and travel back to Maryland. "It wasn't me, it was

Peter Friedman,
later known as Peter Still

the Lord!" she answered. "I always told him, 'I trust you...I expect you to lead me,' and He always did."

William Still also recorded the story of former slave Peter Friedman, perhaps his most remarkable interview. Friedman was from Alabama and came to Still's office in early 1850. When he was just six years old, he had been taken from his family. Forty years later, with the help of a white man, Joseph Friedman, he was able to buy his freedom. Now he was looking for information on his parents. Friedman's story seemed oddly familiar to Still. Friedman told Still his parents' names and where he had first been a slave.

"Suppose I should tell you that I am your brother?" Still asked.

Friedman was surely surprised by the revelation, so Still explained. Friedman had been born while their parents were slaves. Still was born several years later, after their parents had escaped. Their father had died. Still arranged a reunion for Peter with their eighty-year-old mother, their five brothers, and three sisters. Shortly after the reunion Friedman changed his name to Peter Still.

One of the greatest challenges for runaways was to know whom to trust. Harriet Tubman began her journeys in Maryland, traveled through either Wilmington, Delaware, or Philadelphia, and connected only with known stationmasters. But fugitives without her or some other experienced guide were sometimes taken in by phony agents.

In 1853 Robert Jackson and three others escaped slavery in Virginia, but they didn't have a conductor to lead them to safety. Jackson told William Still of his frightening experience with a phony Railroad agent.

When the four fugitives reached Terrytown, Maryland, they met a man who, Jackson said, "talked like a Quaker." The Quakers were peace-loving, and many of them were abolitionists. The man "urged us to go with him to his barn for protection." He fed Jackson and the others breakfast and told them to wait there until nightfall, when he would lead them to Pennsylvania. The men were resting when eight armed men entered the barn. There was a fight. Shots were fired. Jackson's injuries were so severe that he was left behind and held prisoner. "For three days," he told Still, "I was crazy and they thought I would die." But he recovered and somehow got a rope and some nails. He told Still of his escape. "I fastened my nails in under the window sill; tied my rope to the nails, threw my shoes out of the window, put the rope in my mouth, then took hold of it with my well hand, clambered into the window, very weak, but I managed to let myself down to the ground." His three friends had been taken to Baltimore, where they were each sold for twelve hundred dollars. But Jackson was free.

When he recovered from his injuries, Jackson moved to Canada. There he became a brakeman on the Great Western Railroad, a real railroad with tracks and trains. William Still joked that Jackson had been "promoted from the U.G.R.R." (Under Ground Rail Road). But surely even without tracks and trains, no real railroad served its passengers better than the famed U.G.R.R.

Chapter Six

THE FUGITIVE SLAVE LAW

I wouldn't trust Uncle Sam
with my people no longer.
—Harriet Tubman, after the passage
of the Fugitive Slave Law

HARRIET TUBMAN DIDN'T know it in 1850, her first
full year in Philadelphia, but trouble for her and thousands
of slaves desperate to escape was brewing at the Texas-Mexico
border.

In December 1845 the former Mexican territory of Texas
joined the nation as its thirty-eighth state. Texas claimed the
Rio Grande as its western boundary. Mexico claimed the line
was farther east, by the Nueces River. The dispute led to war.

Fighting in what became known as the Mexican War
began in April 1846. Opponents of the conflict considered
it little more than a "land grab" by a powerful country, the
United States. Some thought Southerners were looking to add
more land to grow cotton, and more slave-state votes in Congress to support Southern interests. Among the young offi-

cers in the fighting were George McClellan, Ulysses S. Grant, and Robert E. Lee, who would meet again in the Civil War. By September 1847 U.S. troops took Mexico City, the enemy's capital. By October the war was won.

With the terms of the peace treaty the territory of the United States was greatly expanded. The Rio Grande was recognized as the boundary between Texas and Mexico. The 1.2 million square miles

Horrors of the Fugitive Slave Law

that were added to the United States would become the states of New Mexico, Utah, Nevada, California, and parts of Arizona, Colorado, Kansas, and Wyoming.

Americans wondered what would happen with all this added territory. Would it be slave or free?

In September 1850 Congress compromised on the issue. The new territory would be divided—some would be slave and some would be free. Also, by the terms of the Compromise, there would be no slave trade in the nation's capital, and there would be a strong new fugitive-slave law. It was this new law that meant trouble for Harriet Tubman.

By the terms of the Fugitive Slave Law, anyone accused of being a runaway could be brought before a federal commissioner. The accused was not allowed to testify in his own defense. The commissioner would be paid ten dollars if the accused was returned to slavery but only five dollars if he was freed, a clear attempt to influence the judgment. In addition, all U.S. citizens, even those in free states, were now legally required to turn in runaways. Anyone who refused could be heavily fined. With the passage of this new law, runaways and even legally free blacks were in danger of being arrested.

African Americans bought guns. They formed nighttime patrols on the lookout for slave catchers. Thousands fled north to Canada.

The 1850s were a terrifying time for fugitive slaves and free blacks. Surely Harriet Tubman was frightened. Anyone who suspected she was a runaway was required to turn her in.

James Hamlet was the first African American taken under the new law. He was arrested in New York. Closer to Tubman's new home, Adam Gibson, a free black living in Philadelphia, was arrested and sent into slavery. Just north of the city, Thomas Hall and his wife were taken in the middle of the night, beaten and enslaved.

There were many other arrests.

The law even had a harmful effect on free Northern whites. Ralph Waldo Emerson of Massachusetts, the poet, essayist, and clergyman, said in an 1854 speech, "I had never

Ralph Waldo Emerson

in my life up to this time suffered from the slave institution.... Slavery in Virginia or Carolina was like slavery in Africa or the Fijis for me." But this new law required him to hunt slaves. He called it "a filthy enactment" and declared he would not obey it.

Calvin Fairbank, a clergyman born in New York, was arrested twice for helping African Americans escape. Each time, he was sentenced to a prison term of fifteen years. The first time he was convicted was before the passage of the Fugitive Slave Law, and he was released after four years. In 1852 he was convicted again and held for the next twelve years in a Kentucky prison.

There were battles, too. In September 1851 blacks fought slave catchers near the eastern border of Lancaster, Pennsylvania. One of the slave catchers was killed. A few were wounded. Amazingly, while some of the blacks had bullet holes in their hats, shirts, and boots, none was seriously hurt.

Editorials in Philadelphia newspapers railed against those who defied the law. "It is an act of insurrection," one paper wrote, and they were "in the attitude of levying war against the United States." Another paper declared the defense of fugitives to be "a foul stain upon the fair name and fame of our state." Abolitionists declared it was the Fugitive Slave Law that was to be blamed for the killing near Lancaster, not the runaways and their defenders.

THE LIBERATOR.

Reaction to the Fugitive Slave Law in the October 4, 1850

Issue of William Lloyd Garrison's Newspaper

The Slave-Catching Law.
Boston, Mass.

It is impossible to describe the anguish, terror and despair which all the minds of our colored fellow a citizens (whether Wood or free, but especially of the post-fugitives), in view of the passage of the indescribably cruel Fugitive Slave Bill by Congress… we rejoice to learn that there is a very Strong and almost universal expression or detestation of the Fugitive Bill on the part of our citizens, many of whom openly avow their readiness and fixed purpose to prevent its operation here, even though blood should flow like water…

Affaire in Pittsburg Fugitive Slaves. Pittsburg, Sept. 25. The excitement increases among our colored population in regard to the fugitive slave law. Nearly all the waiters in the hotels have fled to Canada. Sunday, thirty fled; on Monday, forty; on Tuesday, fifty; on Wednesday, thirty; and up to this time, the number that has left will not fall short of three hundred. They went in large bodies, armed with pistols and bowie knives, determined to die rather than be cultured.

NY, Oct. 2. **The Fugitive Slave Excitement.** CA meeting, of the colored population, was held last evening, relative to the fugitive slave law. Strong resolutions were passed, declaring their intention to maintain their rights at all hazards.

Reprinted in *The Liberator* from the *New York Tribune*. **SLAVE CATCHING IN NEW FORE-FIRST CASE UNDER THE LAW.**

The following case, which occurred yesterday, is one of peculiar interest, from the fact of its being the first movement under the new Fugitive Slave Law… Before Commissioner Gardiner: Jones Hamlet, was charged to be a fugitive slave, the property of Mary Brown of Baltimore. No person was present as counsel for accused. Gustavus Brown was sworn in and stated, I am 25 years of age; reside in New York; clerk with A.M. Fenday, 25 Front; resided in New York before coming here in Baltimore; I know James Hamlet; I have known him since a boy; he is a slave to my mother; he is a slave for life…my mother is still entitled to possession of him; she never has parted with him; the man sitting here (Hamlet) is the man…The necessary papers were made out by the Commissioner, Mr. Clare swearing he feared a rescue, and Hamlet was delivered to him, thence to the U.S. Marshal, and probably was conveyed with all possible dispatch to Baltimore, a coach being in waiting at the door; and he was taken off in irons, an officer accompanying the party.

DEATH TO KIDNAPPERS.

(Ohio) Sept. 19, 1850.

I am in the anniversary meeting of the Western A. S. Society. Abby K. Foster is addressing the audience. This is the third and last day of the meeting. It has been a meeting of deep interest. The fugitive slave bill recently passed by Congress has been a principal topic of remark. Ohio is a border State, and fugitive slaves are here and there all over it. There is a settled purpose on the part of these fugitives to defend themselves against all who shall attempt to re-enslave them…If ever a government declared war against its subjects, Congress, by that act, has waged an open, exterminating war against the people of the free States. There is not another government on earth that would dare to record on its statute books such a law…The passage of the fugitive law, by Congress, has roused a spirit in Ohio which will not down at the bidding of government. Slaves are crossing this State daily on their way to Canada. Thousands are taking them by the hand and saying to them 'Stop here; we will protect you; and you shall be taken back to bonds only over our dead bodies.'…Yours, in resisting tyranny, even unto death.

The meeting was addressed by several fugitives and citizens, among them was the venerable Dr. Osgood, who made some remarks against them…and pledged himself to do all in his power to defeat its application and protect fugitives. Resolutions were adopted, declaring the "Bill" unconstitutional and urging an organization against it, and declaring no fugitive shall be carried to Springfield. A large committee of safety was appointed. It is supposed the meeting will adjourn until to-morrow night. People have been standing or squatting about the streets all day. Nothing else talked of.

As a result of the Lancaster battle, thirty men were arrested. After three months in jail they were brought to trial and found to be not guilty. The defense attorney was Congressman Thaddeus Stevens, a champion of abolition. With the court victory, "Underground Rail Road stock rose rapidly," Still later wrote, "and a feeling of universal rejoicing pervaded the friends of freedom from one end of the country to the other."

The Fugitive Slave Law didn't deter Harriet Tubman. Just two months after its passage, John Bowley, a ship carpenter, contacted her. He was a free African American married to Tubman's niece Kessiah, a slave who along with her two children were about to be sold.

It was just one year since Tubman's escape. Legally she was still the property of Eliza Brodess. Travel for her was especially dangerous. Nonetheless, she snuck back to Maryland with Bowley. She stayed in Baltimore with Tom Tubman, her husband's brother. There she and Bowley made plans to help Kessiah and her children escape. Tubman would wait for them in Baltimore and lead them to the free state of Pennsylvania.

On the day of the sale, Bowley was in the crowd by the steps of the Cambridge, Maryland, courthouse waiting for the auction to begin. At the time, for many people in the South, a slave auction was good, free entertainment. Onlookers gathered with drinks and smokes, and hooted and cheered as slaves were brought to the steps of the courthouse.

Kessiah was young and healthy. Her two children were proof she was fertile, and that whoever bought her could expect her to give birth to many more slaves. The bidding started and the price for Kessiah and her children went higher and higher. In the end it was Bowley who gave the highest bid, but by then it was time for lunch. Before the sale could be completed, the auctioneer took a break. When he returned to the courthouse he expected the winning bidder to pay for his slaves, but Bowley had disappeared. The sale was voided and the bidding started again for Kessiah and her children until someone realized that they were gone, too!

Thaddeus Stevens

John Bowley and his wife and children were hiding in a house near the courthouse. It was December and nightfall came early. When it was dark they snuck down to the nearby icy Choptank River and onto a small boat Bowley had hidden there. They sailed northwest to Chesapeake Bay on their way to Baltimore, a trip of seventy-five miles. When they arrived in Baltimore, Kessiah's Aunt Harriet greeted them. A few nights later she led them to Philadelphia.

In the spring of 1851, just a few months after Tubman helped Kessiah escape, she returned to Maryland yet again. This time she helped her brother Moses and two other runaways make their way north.

By the fall, after two years in Philadelphia, Tubman had a furnished room and some money saved. She made plans to bring her husband north. She bought him a suit of clothes and again risked her freedom by slipping back to Dorchester County, Maryland.

When she arrived she sent a message telling him where

Baltimore, Maryland,
1840

they could meet. She got a shocking reply: John Tubman refused to join her. During her absence he had married someone else, a woman named Caroline.

Harriet was furious. She had traveled more than one hundred miles and had risked everything for him. At first she was determined to confront her husband even if it meant she would be captured and returned to slavery. But she had second thoughts. "How foolish it was," she told herself, "just for temper to make mischief." She decided, "If he could do without her, she could do without him." She said later that at that moment he "dropped out" of her heart. Still, she kept to her Christian values. There may have been no place in her heart for John Tubman, but for the sixteen more years he remained alive she didn't remarry.

Chapter Seven

"SHOUT, YOU ARE FREE!"

I've served my master all my days,
Without a dime reward,
And now I'm forced to run away,
To flee the lash, abroad.
—From a song Tubman and those with her
sang as they fled north in 1856

IN DECEMBER 1851, a few months after her failed attempt to bring her husband north, Harriet Tubman returned to Dorchester County. This time she led eleven slaves, members of her family and strangers, all the way to Rochester, New York, near Lake Ontario. Across the lake was slave-free Canada. The runaways traveled only at night and hid at Underground Railroad stops during the day.

One of several Railroad agents in Rochester was Frederick Douglass. He wrote in his autobiography, "On one occasion I had eleven fugitives at the same time under my roof, and it was necessary for them to remain with me, until I could collect sufficient money to get them to Canada." It's likely he was writing of Tubman's runaways. He wrote that they were "well content with very plain food, and a strip of carpet on the floor for a bed, or a place on the straw in the barn loft."

Harriet Tubman's first biographer, Sarah Bradford, wrote in 1869 that she had made a total of nineteen trips south and led three hundred slaves to freedom. Serious historians believe Bradford's numbers were exaggerated, perhaps to make Tubman's story even more compelling. One good reason to doubt the inflated numbers is William Still's 1872 record of the Underground Railroad, an almost eight-hundred-page book retelling the stories of hundreds of fugitive slaves who passed though Philadelphia. He wrote only twice about slaves rescued by Harriet Tubman. Still wrote of her 1854 rescue of her brothers and of her 1857 rescue of her parents. Historians believe Tubman made a total of thirteen trips and brought out seventy slaves. She also gave helpful information to about fifty other slaves intent on escaping slavery.

Most often Tubman traveled in winter, because then nights were long, dark, and cold, and people who might report runaways were likely to be indoors huddled by their fireplaces. After each trip she returned to the Northeast and usually worked until the next winter. The money she earned helped finance her trips south.

"Hail, oh hail ye happy spirits," she sang to let people know she was there and ready. "Moses go down in Egypt. Tell ole Pharaoh let me go."

In 1854 she was ready to help her enslaved brothers to escape. She had someone write a letter and send it to a free black man who lived in Dorchester County. "Tell my brothers," was written near the end of the letter, "when the good old ship of Zion comes along, to be ready to step aboard." They would meet at the corncrib by their father's cabin.

She arrived in late December, just in time to save them.

They were scheduled to be sold the next day at a public auction.

Henry, Ben, Ben's fiancée Jane Kane, and two other slaves, John Chase and Peter Jackson, met Tubman as planned. But Robert didn't come. His wife, Mary Manokey, was about to have a baby, their third child. Robert knew his wife needed him, but he also knew that if he stayed too long he would be sold and probably sent far away. Robert Ross waited. He stayed with his wife until their daughter was born. They named her Harriet. Then, when he thought his wife was asleep, he started to leave. His wife stirred in her bed and called to him. Robert didn't have the heart to say he was running away, leaving her with three young children, so he told her he was going to look for work. It's doubtful she believed him. It was early Christmas morning, no time to find a job.

Just before daybreak Robert Ross arrived at Ben Ross's corncrib.

When Tubman and the others were settled in, Chase and Jackson went to the cabin and told Ben Ross that his children were outside. Ross brought them food. Several times during the day he checked on them, but he never looked directly at his children. He knew that after they were gone, slave catchers would come and ask if he had seen them. He wanted to be able to truthfully say that he hadn't.

It was Christmas and Rit Green had expected Ben, Henry, and Robert for dinner. She had roasted a pig and cooked vegetables. Her children watched from their hiding place as their mother came out of the cabin, shaded her eyes, and looked down the road for them, but they didn't come out.

This was the first time in more than five years that

Harriet Tubman had seen her mother, but she was afraid to let her know she was there and to take the chance that her mother would make a fuss and try to stop her and the others from going. The four Ross children left that night without ever speaking to their mother.

Four days later they arrived in Wilmington, Delaware, at the house of Thomas Garrett. It was a difficult journey. Garrett's letter to another agent of the Railroad implies they walked the whole way. Garrett wrote, "Harriet and one of the men had worn their shoes off their feet, and I gave them two dollars to help fit them out." He helped get them onto a carriage and sent them north to an agent's house in Pennsylvania.

Thomas Garrett

Once they were free, Tubman's brothers changed their names, probably to elude slave hunters. They took the last name Stewart, the surname of one of the leading white families in Dorchester County. Ben became James Stewart. Robert became John Stewart, and Henry became William Henry Stewart. Tubman led her brothers, Jane Kane, Chase, and Jackson to Saint Catharines, Ontario.

"Shout," she told them when they crossed the border into Canada. "Shout, you are free!"

Harriet Tubman stayed in Saint Catharines through the spring and summer. In October 1855 she returned to Philadelphia and then back to Dorchester County. She was determined to rescue her sister Rachel Ross.

More and more slaves had been running off, and slaveholders had become more alert, making it even more difficult to escape. Tubman waited for three months for the chance to free her sister, but Rachel was not able to break away with

Reverend Samuel Green

Harriet Beecher Stowe

her two children, so Tubman returned to Philadelphia.

In May 1857 she went back for her elderly parents. There was a sense of urgency to her mission. Her friend Reverend Samuel Green, a free black who was an agent of the Railroad, had been arrested and charged with helping a group of fugitive slaves. The Dorchester County sheriff had searched Green's house and found railroad schedules, letters from fugitives, and a copy of Harriet Beecher Stowe's novel *Uncle Tom's Cabin*, an 1852 best-selling book that exposed the horrors of American slavery to millions of readers in the United States and overseas. For owning that book, which was illegal in Maryland, Reverend Green was sentenced to ten years in prison. Tubman's parents had helped the same runaways as Green. There was a rumor they would be arrested, too.

Tubman's parents were no longer slaves. Her father had been freed in 1840 at his slaveholder's death by the terms of his will. In 1855 he had bought his wife's freedom. She was already an old woman, so the price was nominal. Tubman's parents were free but lonely. Much of their family had escaped to Canada. And now they were in danger of being arrested. They had to leave Maryland, and they needed someone to lead them.

There was danger, of course, for Tubman. She was still a fugitive slave. Her previous rescues were in the winter when the nights were long, but this was late May, a difficult time to travel without being seen. Harriet Green and Ben Ross were in their seventies and couldn't walk their way north.

Nonetheless, she was determined to save them.

When she got to them, she found that her father wanted to take along some of his tools. Her mother wanted to take some bedding. Tubman told them they had to leave everything behind.

Tubman bought an old horse and put together a primitive wagon so her parents could ride. When they reached the railroad her parents got on board a train and Tubman took the horse.

When at last Tubman's parents reached Philadelphia they met with William Still. They told him of their years in slavery. They spoke with great regret of their children who had been sold and taken to Georgia. Ross spoke of his master, who was "a wolf in sheep's clothing," a minister "pretending to preach for twenty years."

Report from
The National Era
An African-American Newspaper
APRIL 1, 1852

UNCLE TOM'S CABIN.

Mrs. Stowe has at last brought her great work to a close. The last chapters appear in this week's *Era*. With our consent, the Boston publishers issued an edition of five thousand on the 20th of March, but it has already been exhausted, and another edition of five thousand has appeared. We do not recollect any production of an American writer that has excited more profound and general interest. Since the commencement of its publication in our columns, we have received literally thousands of testimonials from our renewing subscribers, to its unsurpassed ability. We hope that this grand work of fiction may not be the last service to be rendered by Mrs. Stowe to the cause of Freedom, through the columns of the *National Era*...

William Still wrote with some admiration, "They seemed delighted at the idea of going to a free country.... Not many of those thus advanced in years ever succeeded in getting to Canada."

❧

In her travels, Harriet Tubman had many adventures. One of the most frightening was when she came to the house of a friend, a free black who was an agent of the Railroad. She knocked on the front door with her secret code and waited. When no one answered, she knocked again.

"Who are you?" a white man shouted from a window. "What do you want?"

The man she had come to see no longer lived there. He had been chased out for harboring runaways. Tubman knew she had to get away fast. She led her party of fugitives to a small island in the middle of a swamp. They hid there in the tall, wet grass until nightfall, when a white man, probably a Quaker, came walking along the edge of the swamp. He seemed to be talking to himself.

"My wagon stands in the barnyard of the next farm across the way," he said. "The horse is in the stable; the harness hangs on a nail."

After nightfall Tubman and the others went to the farm and found the wagon. It was loaded with enough food to feed them all. They took the wagon to the next town, to the house of an agent she knew.

Tubman never questioned how the man knew they were hiding in the swamp. She had prayed for deliverance, and was never surprised when it came. "I'm going to hold steady on to You," she said in her prayers, "and You've got to see me through."

On another trip north she had a premonition of danger. "Children," she told her group, "we must stop here and cross the river." It was a wide, fast-running river. She didn't know how deep the water was, but she stepped in. The others waited. Once they saw she had safely made it across, they followed.

"The water never came above my chin," Tubman said. "When we thought surely we were all going under, it became shallower and shallower, and we came out safe on the other side."

She found out later that reward notices for the runaways had been posted just a short way ahead on their original route. And near the notices were slave catchers waiting for them. Her premonition had saved them. When she was asked about it she said, "It wasn't me. It was the Lord!"

Chapter Eight

JOHN BROWN

When I think how he gave up his life
for our people…it's clear to me
it wasn't mortal man, it was God in him.
—Harriet Tubman, on the death of John Brown

FOR THREE DAYS in January 1858 Harriet Tubman stayed with Frederick Douglass and his wife, Anna Murray, in Rochester, New York. She impressed them with stories of her adventures. During her visit Douglass wrote in a letter to a friend that Harriet Tubman "possesses great courage and shrewdness."

Just after she left, Douglass and Murray had another visitor, John Brown of Connecticut.

Brown was tall and lanky with a narrow face and a long, tangled beard. Atop his head was an impressive mop of unkempt hair. Henry David Thoreau said, "He was a man of Spartan habit. Scrupulous about his diet at your table, excusing himself by saying that he must eat sparingly and fare hard as became a soldier." He was a formidable, intense man, deeply opposed to slavery.

Report from
The National Era
An African-American Newspaper
OCTOBER 27, 1859

A LONG CONVERSATION WITH **BROWN**.

The reporter of the Baltimore *American* furnishes the following interesting account of a conversation between Senator Mason (of Virginia) and others and **Brown**, the leader of the revolt…After some little delay, we were introduced into the room where **Brown** and Stevens lay. We found the former to be a six-footer, although as he lay he had the appearance of being some six inches shorter than that. He has a rather peculiar shaped head long gray hair, which at this time was matted, the sabre cut in his head having caused blood to flow freely, to the complete disfigurement of his face, which, like his hands, was begrimed with dirt, evidently the result of continued exposure to the smoke of powder. His eyes are of a pale blue, or perhaps a sharp gray…During his conversation, hereafter reported, no sign of weakness was exhibited…The language of Governor Wise well expresses his boldness, when he said, "He is the gamest man I ever saw."…

Brown. I think, my friend, you are guilty of a great wrong against God and humanity. I say that without wishing to be offensive. It would be perfectly right for any one to interfere with you, so far as to free those you willfully and wickedly hold in bondage. I do not say this insultingly.

Mr. Mason. I understand that.

Brown. I think I did right, and that others will do right who interfere with you at any time, and all times. I hold that the golden rule, do unto others as you would that others should do unto you, applies to all who would help others to gain their liberty…

Q. Where did you get arms?

Brown. I bought them.

Q. In what State?

Brown. That I would not tell.

…A SPEECH TO THE REPORTERS. Mr. **Brown** here made a statement, intended for the reporters of the *Baltimore American*, *Cincinnati Gazette*, and *N.Y. Herald*, who were present, as follows:…I claim to be here in carrying out a measure I believe to be perfectly justifiable, and not to act the part of an incendiary or ruffian; but, on the contrary, to aid those suffering under a great wrong. I wish to say, further, that you had better, all you people of the South, prepare yourselves for a settlement of this question. It must come up for settlement sooner than you are prepared for it, and the sooner you commence that preparation the better for you. You may dispose of me very easily; I am nearly disposed of now; but this question is still to be settled…The end is not yet…We did kill some when defending ourselves, but I saw no one fire except directly in self-defence. Our orders were strict not to harm any one not in arms against us.

Q. Well, **Brown**, suppose you had all the negroes in the United States, what would you do with them?

Brown (in a loud tone, and with emphasis). Set them free, sir!…

Brown claimed his family was among the original Pilgrim settlers. He had been an agent for the Underground Railroad in Pennsylvania. In 1855 he and five of his sons moved to Kansas and became active there in the anti-slavery movement. They hoped Kansas would join the Union as a free state.

Brown took his anti-slavery passion to a violent extreme. He pulled people he suspected of being pro-slavery from their homes and killed them. One of his sons died in his anti-slavery battles. Another was arrested and driven insane in prison.

Brown told Douglass he had a plan to defeat slavery. He would gather a small army that would capture the arsenal at Harper's Ferry, Virginia, now West Virginia. With the weapons and ammunition from the arsenal he would fight the U.S. Army and capture even more weapons. He hoped to enlist Douglass's help.

"Come with me," Brown told Douglass. "I want you for a special purpose. When I strike, the bees will begin to swarm, and I shall need you to help hive them." Brown's "bees" were African Americans, and he was sure they would rally around Douglass.

Douglass doubted the wisdom of the plan. He later wrote, "My discretion or my cowardice made me proof against the old man's eloquence....Some have thought that I ought to have gone with him, but I have no reproaches for myself at this point." He added that the people who criticized him for not joining Brown were other African Americans who also were not at Harper's Ferry, so "I shall not trouble myself about their criticisms."

In April 1858, three months after her visit at Douglass's

Harper's Ferry, 1840

house, Harriet Tubman was back in St. Catharines. Jermaine Loguen, a minister, onetime slave, and agent of the Underground Railroad, said that John Brown would like to come to her house to meet her.

Tubman was not surprised. She told Loguen, "I knew he was coming."

She had dreamed several times that she was in a "wilderness sort of place, all rocks and bushes," when she saw a large snake. "While I looked, it changed into the head of an old man with a long white beard." Just as the old man was about to speak, two younger heads appeared beside him. Then a great

John Brown

many men came. They struck the two young men and then they struck the bearded man.

Now she was certain the old man in her dreams was John Brown.

Brown entered her house, and she was struck by how much he resembled her vision. They shook hands and made an immediate connection. She called him "Captain" Brown and he called her "General" Tubman. He asked her to raise funds for his mission and encourage former slaves then living in Canada to join him, and she said she would. They met again, a few months later, but Brown's scheduled raid was delayed. Communication at the time was not always easy, and they lost touch with each other.

After his meeting with Tubman, Brown went to Kansas, Pennsylvania, Massachusetts, and New York to raise money and troops for the raid on Harper's Ferry. Surely many people doubted his plan could succeed. All this resistance caused Brown to delay the attack until October 1859, a full year and a half after his first meeting with Tubman.

Meanwhile, she busied herself with her parents. Her mother wasn't comfortable in Saint Catharines, and in the spring of 1859 they moved back to the United States, to Auburn, New York.

Why Auburn? On her many trips from Pennsylvania to Canada, Tubman surely passed through Auburn, a town between Syracuse and Rochester noted for its strong anti-slavery sentiment. When she was there it's likely she met with some of the women active in the abolitionist movement, including Frances Miller Seward, the wife of United States Senator and former New York governor William Henry Seward. Early in 1859 Seward sold Tubman a seven-acre farm in Auburn with a house, a barn, and a few smaller sheds. The terms of the sale were reasonable, a down payment of twenty-five dollars and four payments a year of just ten dollars each over the next thirty years.

With her parents settled, Tubman left Auburn and went to Boston and looked for personal support and help for the refugee community. There she met Franklin Benjamin Sanborn, a schoolmaster and newspaper editor who was fascinated by her stories. He introduced her to many of the abolitionist leaders living in the area, including William Lloyd Garrison and Wendell Phillips. They were all anxious to meet the courageous, famous Harriet Tubman.

They came to meet her at her boardinghouse, but they were strangers to her and she was still a fugitive. To be sure her visitors were not there to trap her, she showed them daguerreotypes—an early form of photographs—of her abolitionist friends. If they could identify the people in the daguerreotypes she let them in.

She charmed her visitors. She told them of her enslavement and her escape. Her sessions were like one-woman plays. When she quoted other people she imitated them. And she sang the songs she used to let slaves know she was about to travel north. She told them of her misadventure with her husband, how she had prepared to bring him north with a new suit but he wouldn't go. "I had his clothes," she said, "but no husband."

According to Sanborn, with these meetings Tubman raised

"a handsome sum of money toward the payment of her debt to Mr. Seward."

In August 1859 she spoke in Boston at the New England Colored Citizens' Convention. She was introduced as "one of the most successful conductors on the Underground Railroad." At the time, some leaders of the African-American community had understandably soured on the United States and proposed that they all leave the country and move to Haiti or Africa. Tubman was against this. She said white people had blacks do their hardest work and now they wanted them to leave. "They can't do it," she said. "We're rooted here, and they can't pull us up."

In May 1859, during her stay in Boston, she met again with John Brown. She helped him collect money for his cause. Brown introduced her to his supporters as "one of the best and bravest persons on this continent."

There were reports at the time that someone traveled about in disguise trying to recruit people to join Brown. Some people think it was Harriet Tubman. There are also reports that she was sure his plan was doomed to fail, and pretended to be too ill to join him.

In July, Brown assumed the name John Smith and rented a farmhouse five miles from the United States arsenal at Harper's Ferry. On Sunday night, October 16, 1859, he led a raid on the arsenal. He freed slaves, took hostages, and captured a huge supply of rifles and ammunition. In the North, news of the attack created excitement among many who were unsympathetic to slavery. In the South, people were terrified that this was just the beginning of a widespread conspiracy intent on ending slavery.

When the local militia could not defeat Brown and the more than twenty men who had joined him, the Marines were called in. They arrived two days after the first attack. They were led by Colonel Robert E. Lee, the man who would soon lead the rebellious Confederate army. One of his soldiers was John Wilkes Booth, the man who one day would murder President Lincoln. Five of Brown's men somehow escaped. Ten were killed, including two of Brown's sons and two of the slaves he had freed. Seven others, including John Brown, were captured.

Brown was tried for murder, treason, and inciting slaves to revolt.

"He needed no babbling lawyer, making false issues to defend him," Henry David Thoreau said in a speech in 1859. "He could not have been tried by a jury of his peers, because his peers did not exist."

"I have, may it please the court, a few words to say," Brown said at his trial. He told the court how in the past he had led slaves to Canada. Then he explained his intentions at Harper's Ferry. "I designed to have done the same thing again, on a larger scale. That was all I intended to do. I never did intend murder, or treason, or the destruction of property, or to excite or incite the slaves to rebellion, or to make insurrection."

John Brown was found guilty.

On November 18, Mary Day Brown passed through Worcester, Massachusetts, on her way to visit her husband. She told a reporter that she had thirteen children but only four survived, and she "would willingly see the ruin of all her household, if it would only help the cause of freedom."

She didn't reach her husband in time to see him before his hanging. On November 30 Brown wrote to his family, "Be of good cheer, and believe and trust in God with all your heart, and with all your soul; for He doeth all things well." Just before his execution he wrote that he was "quite certain

John Brown besieged at Harper's Ferry

that the crimes of this guilty land will never be purged away but with blood."

John Brown was hanged on December 2, 1859.

Prominent politicians, including Abraham Lincoln, condemned Brown's raid, but Southern whites believed the Northern politicians regretted only that the revolt had failed. They felt they would have to create a separate nation or lose their right to have slaves.

"For a year or more after the Harper's Ferry battle," William Still wrote later, "the mob spirit of the times was very violent in all the principal northern cities, as well as southern.... Even in Boston, Abolition meetings were fiercely assailed by the mob."

Harriet Tubman was bewildered by Brown's dedication to the abolition of slavery. "She had often risked her own life for her people," Sanborn wrote in 1863, "but that a white man, and a man so noble and strong, should so take upon himself the burden of a despised race, she could not understand." But she admired him. "He done more in dying," Harriet Tubman told a friend, "than a hundred men would in living."

When news of the raid on Harper's Ferry reached her, she felt she finally understood all of her prophetic dream. When she had first met Brown she recognized him as the old man in her dream with the long white beard. In her dream, a great many men did come after him and in the end kill him. Now she felt she also knew the identities of the two young men with him. They were Brown's sons Watson and Oliver, and as in her dream they had been killed, too.

View from Mount Ida, near Troy, New York

Chapter Nine

A MIRACULOUS
RESCUE

Go it, old Aunty!
You're the best old aunty the fellow ever had.
—A small boy's cry when Harriet Tubman was running
with Charles Nalle toward the river

IN APRIL 1860 Harriet Tubman was on her way from her home in Auburn to Boston to attend an anti-slavery meeting. She stopped in Troy, New York, where she planned to visit a cousin. While there she heard that Charles Nalle, a fugitive slave, had been arrested and was about to be sent back to Virginia.

Nalle was in the U.S. commissioner's office at the corner of First and State streets. The city's African Americans and anti-slavery activists were enraged, and gathered there. By the time Tubman arrived, the corner was jammed with a noisy crowd of people and horse-drawn wagons. Through a window they saw Nalle on the second story. His wrists were locked in chains.

Tubman wrapped a shawl around herself and pulled

down the brim of her sunbonnet so her face was hidden. She hunched her shoulders and limped to the entrance of the commissioner's office. Since she seemed old and harmless, she was let inside. The people outside saw her through the window. They recognized her and whispered that "Moses" had arrived.

Nalle and two police officers walked toward the stairs. At the bottom of the stairway they met Tubman. "Here they come!" she yelled.

"Take him!" someone else shouted, and the crowd responded.

In the midst of all this someone yelled, "Fire!" which only added to the confusion.

Tubman bent down and charged at the police officer who was holding Nalle. She threw him to the ground and shouted, "Give us liberty or give us death!"

One of the police officers hit her with his club. She fought back. Then she grabbed Nalle. "Drag him to the river," she called out. "Drown him but don't let them have him!"

Perhaps this reflected how she felt about her own freedom, that she would rather die than be sent back to slavery.

Tubman held on to Nalle as the police knocked them down. According to one newspaper report, they were pushed to the ground twenty times, and every time they went down Tubman pulled Nalle up. She wouldn't give in and she wouldn't let go.

At last, with the help of the crowd, Tubman and Nalle made their way to the waterfront and boarded a boat and set out across the Hudson River. The police officers boarded a ferry and the chase went on.

When the boat and ferry reached the other side of the river the police once again grabbed the still-chained Nalle. They took him to a judge's office. The anti-slavery crowd had followed them, and threw stones. The police fired their guns.

Then a huge African American named Martin rushed toward the building. One of the officers hit him with a hatchet and the big man fell across the doorway, keeping the police from closing the door. The crowd ran in behind him and rescued Nalle. Tubman and some other women led the tired and bloodied Nalle to a wagon, which would take him on his journey north to Canada. Nalle was free again.

Nalle's two chief rescuers disappeared. Martin recovered quickly, and then he and Tubman ran off.

Harriet Tubman continued to Boston.

She spent the spring and summer of 1860 in New England working with anti-slavery leaders there, among them some of the great intellectuals of her time, such as Ralph Waldo Emerson, Horace Mann, and Wendell Phillips.

In late November she snuck back into Dorchester County, determined to finally rescue her sister Rachel and Rachel's children Angerine and Ben. But it was too late. Rachel died shortly before she arrived.

Tubman sent her niece Angerine and nephew Ben a message. They should meet her at a certain section of a nearby forest. It was a windy and snowy night. Tubman hid behind a tree and waited, but Rachel's children never came.

She was disappointed, but she wasn't alone when she left Maryland. Stephen Ennets, whose slaveholder kept him apart from his wife and children, found her. She led him, his wife Maria, their three children, and another fugitive to freedom.

Horace Mann

Wendell Phillips

Gerrit Smith

On December 1, 1860, her friend Thomas Garrett of Wilmington, Delaware, wrote to William Still about this mission. "I write to let you know that Harriet Tubman is again in these parts. She arrived last evening from one of her trips of mercy to God's poor, bringing two men with her as far as New Castle...the wife of one of the men, with two or three children, was left some thirty miles below." She had come to Garrett for some money so she could hire a carriage to take them. "I shall be very uneasy about them, till I hear they are safe. There is now much more risk on the road," Garrett wrote, "than there has been for several months past...yet, as it is Harriet who seems to have a special angel to guard her on her journey of mercy, I have hope."

They did arrive safely in Philadelphia. Then she led the group to Canada.

In January 1861 she went to Peterboro, New York, and stayed with the prominent white abolitionist Gerrit Smith and his family. But soon after she arrived there was frightening news from Auburn. A slave catcher had come to town hoping to capture fugitive slaves and take them down south. She hurried back to Canada.

Her November rescue of the seven slaves including the Ennets family was her last trip south before the Civil War.

Chapter Ten

SECESSION

They say the Negro has no rights
but it seems to me they send men to Congress
and pay them eight dollars a day
for nothing else but to talk about the Negro.
—Harriet Tubman, talking just before the Civil War
about the national obsession with the issue of slavery

IN 1857 THE SUPREME COURT, led by Chief Justice Roger Taney, a former slave owner, ruled that no African American descended from a slave could be a citizen. The court also ruled that Congress had no right to exclude slavery from any of the territories. Slaveholders were delighted. Those against slavery were outraged.

In January 1857 anti-slavery activists held a Disunion Convention in Worcester, Massachusetts, at which William Lloyd Garrison and other speakers called for free states to break away from slave states. In 1857 it was the anti-slavery activists who proposed secession.

"We are two peoples," the *New-York Tribune* declared in an editorial. "We are a people for Freedom and a people for Slavery...conflict is inevitable."

Abraham Lincoln

In 1860 William Seward, the senator and former governor of New York who had sold Harriet Tubman her home in Auburn, campaigned to be the Republican Party nominee for president. But the party chose a former congressman from Illinois, Abraham Lincoln. The Democratic Party was split. The southern half of the party nominated John C. Breckenridge of Kentucky. The northern half nominated Stephen A. Douglas of Illinois. The former Whig and Know-Nothing parties merged and nominated John Bell of Tennessee. And running under the banner of the Radical Abolitionist Party was Harriet Tubman's friend, Gerrit Smith of New York.

The biggest issue of the campaign was slavery. Smith pledged to abolish it, but he had very little chance of being elected. Of the others, Lincoln took the strongest anti-slavery stance. He pledged to tolerate it in the fifteen slave states but not allow it to spread into the territories. Lincoln's promise was too much for Governor William Henry Gist of South Carolina, and he declared that if Lincoln was elected, his state would leave the Union.

During the campaign there were widespread rumors in the South of slave revolts, women and children being murdered, water supplies being poisoned, and whole towns being set on fire. Southerners armed themselves, ready to defend their homes and families.

On November 6, with less that 40 percent of the votes, Lincoln was elected president. Six and a half weeks later, on December 20, the South Carolina legislature met and declared the state no longer part of the United States. The legislatures of Mississippi, Florida, Alabama, Georgia, Louisiana, and Texas soon joined South Carolina. Their representatives met in February 1861 and formed the Confederate States of America, with its capital in Richmond, Virginia. Jefferson Davis of Mississippi was chosen president of the Confederacy and Alexander H. Stephens of Georgia its vice president.

Government officials were afraid of an attack on President-elect Lincoln, so his travel plans from Illinois to the nation's capital were kept secret. He was heavily guarded at his inauguration.

"Apprehension seems to exist among the people of the Southern states," Lincoln said at the beginning of his inaugural address. He reassured the South that he had "no purpose, directly or indirectly, to interfere with the institution of slavery in the states where it exists." He spoke against secession, stating that no state "can lawfully get out of the Union." He declared, "In *your* hands, my dissatisfied fellow-countrymen, and not in *mine*, is the momentous issue of civil war. . . . We are not enemies, but friends."

"They may say, 'Peace, peace!' as much as they like," Tubman said at the time. "I know there is going to be war!"

Forts, arsenals, navy yards, and other property belonging to the federal government but within the rebelling states were seized by the Confederacy. Then, on April 12, people in Charleston Harbor, South Carolina, sat on nearby wharves and rooftops and watched Confederate troops fire on Fort Sumter, a fort occupied by Union troops that was set on a man-made island at the entrance to the harbor. It was a brutal attack.

By the next day the wooden barracks inside the fort were burning. The heat was so intense that the

Confederate flag

Union flag from Fort Sumter

A Confederate flag flies over Fort Sumter, April 14, 1861.

soldiers in it were forced to lie on the ground, their mouths covered with wet cloths. Major Anderson, who commanded the Union troops, later said, "Having defended Fort Sumter for thirty-four hours, until the quarters were entirely burned, the main gates destroyed by fire, the gorge walls seriously injured...with no provisions remaining but pork, I accepted the terms of evacuation offered by General Beauregard."

The Union soldiers were allowed to leave with honor. Miraculously, no one on either side had died in the attack.

News of the fall of Fort Sumter caused a great uproar throughout the country. There was no longer any hope that the dispute would be settled peacefully.

The states of Virginia, Arkansas, North Carolina, and Tennessee withdrew from the Union and joined the Confederacy. Four slaves states, Delaware, Maryland, Kentucky, and Missouri, remained in the Union.

The news of the loss of Fort Sumter reported in the North

In the North American flags were draped out of windows and from rooftops. There were meetings and parades. "The Union must be preserved!" people called out. "To arms!"

President Lincoln called for seventy-five thousand volunteer troops to serve for a period of three months, an indication he expected the fighting to end quickly.

In the South there was a call for thirty-five thousand to volunteer.

Southerners believed people up north didn't really want to fight, that the war was forced upon them by fanatic abolitionists. They felt sure it would be a short war, that they were "invincible by any force the North can send against them." In the North, the feelings were equally strong that this "hell-born rebellion" would be quickly put down.

The North and South were unequally matched. While the territories of the two sides were about the same size, more people lived in the Northern states. According to the 1860 census there were about twenty-two million people living in

The Battle of Bull Run, July 1861

the states that remained in the Union. There were about nine million people in the Confederacy, and about 40 percent of them were slaves.

The Civil War, sometimes called the War of Secession, was fought by great armies, over a broad stretch of territory, with a huge, tragic loss of lives. It tore the nation apart.

In all, more than 2.5 million men fought in the war. There were more than two thousand skirmishes, about 150 of them important enough to be called "battles."

Shortly after the war began, the cry "On to Richmond!" rang through the North, where the hope was that a quick victory against Confederate troops in their capital would end the fighting.

The Union's plan was to take Richmond, blockade the Southern harbors, and control the Mississippi River and thereby split the Southern forces.

The first great fight was near a small stream named Bull Run at Manassas Junction, Virginia. In July 1861 about thirty thousand undisciplined Union troops were led into battle by General Irvin McDowell. It was a Union disaster. Thousands of McDowell's men threw down their guns and ran.

The disaster at Bull Run roused the North. Within a few months more than half a million men joined the Union army. The largest forces were in Washington, and General George B. McClellan was called to command them.

The Union navy fared better than the army. It was successful in blocking ships from reaching Southern ports. Much-needed manufactured goods could not get in, and raw cotton and other Southern products could not get out. In time, the blockade would strangle the South.

In March 1862 two ironclad ships, the Confederates' *Merrimack,* said to look like a "half-submerged barn," and

The Monitor *and the* Merrimack

the Union's *Monitor,* described as a "Yankee cheesebox on a raft," fought a four-hour battle off the coast of Virginia. Each fired cannonballs at the other, some as heavy as two hundred pounds. In the end, both sides withdrew and claimed victory. The battle was a turning point in the war. Wooden fighting ships were now obsolete.

In the spring of 1861, while the nation was preparing for war, Harriet Tubman traveled to New York City and stayed at the house of Henry Highland Garnet, a minister and dedicated abolitionist. Early one morning, Tubman had a startling vision while she slept. She awoke, hurried downstairs, and called out, "My people are free! My people are free!"

"Do cease this noise," Garnet told her. "My grand-children may see the day of emancipation of our people, but neither you nor I."

Tubman was forever confident in her closeness to God. She was sure this was a prophetic dream. She insisted emancipation would come in her lifetime. To the annoyance of Garnet, she sang it out again: "My people are free! My people are free!"

In April or May 1861 she returned to her home in Auburn with a young girl named Margaret Stewart, who she said was her niece. She arranged for the girl to live with Mrs. Lazette Worden, who took her to live with her at her sister's house. Worden's sister Frances was the wife of William Seward, who was now Lincoln's secretary of state. Margaret Stewart was treated as a guest in the Seward house, an elegant home with fashionable furniture, fancy rugs, works of art, and books. This was a rare experience for an African-American girl in the mid–1800s.

Margaret Stewart Lucas and her daughter Alice Stewart Brickler in the 1900s

There are all sorts of conflicting reports on the identity of Margaret Stewart. According to Alice Stewart Brickler, Stewart's daughter, Tubman had kidnapped the girl, and "Secretly and without so much as a by-your-leave, took the little girl with her to her Northern home." At the time it was written that the child had been a slave. Brickler said, "Neither she, her brothers, or her mother had ever been slaves."

Report from

DOUGLASS' MONTHLY
An African-American Newspaper
DECEMBER, 1860

THE LATE ELECTION...No preceding election resembles this in its issues and parties, and none resembles it in the effects it has already produced, and is still likely to produce. It was a contest between sections, North and South, as to what shall be the principles and policy of the national Government in respect to the slave system of the fifteen Southern States...The Northern people have **elected**, against the opposition of the slaveholding South, a man for President who declared his opposition to the further extension of slavery over the soil belonging to the United States. Such is the head and front, and the full extent of the offense, for which 'minute men' are forming, drums are beating, flags are flying, people are arming, 'banks are closing,' 'stocks are falling,' and the South generally taking on dreadfully...Slavery shall be destroyed.

Tubman claimed the girl was her brother's child, but historians cannot determine which brother. Some speculate that Margaret Stewart was Harriet Tubman's secret daughter and had been born before Tubman escaped slavery, then left with a free black woman to raise. Brickler admitted, "Mother looked very much like Aunt Harriet."

Whatever Margaret Stewart's lineage, she was raised in the Seward home, and there, her daughter said, she was taught "to speak properly, to read, write, sew, do housework, and act as a lady."

After leaving the girl with Worden and Seward, Tubman went to Massachusetts to raise money to help support her parents and to continue her work helping the millions of African Americans still held as slaves.

Tubman had strong opinions on slavery and on the war between the states. "Never wound a snake, but kill it," she told her friend the writer and abolitionist Lydia Maria Child. For Tubman, the Confederacy was the snake.

Tubman thought African Americans should be given a major role in the fighting. She argued that by not freeing the

Confederate currency, 1861

U.S. Treasury Note, 1861

slaves so they could join the military, Lincoln was holding back Union victory.

The war brought turmoil to the South. Many slaves ran off, crossing battle lines to the Union side. According to the Fugitive Slave Law, they were to be returned. But some people thought that with secession the rules had changed.

In May 1861 three African Americans who had been the slaves of Confederate Colonel Mallory escaped to Fort Monroe in Virginia, which was then under the command of General

Benjamin F. Butler. Butler told his men to feed the runaways and put them to work. The next day two Confederates held out a flag of truce. They said they had come to take back Mallory's slaves.

"I intend to hold them," Butler said. Virginia had declared it was no longer part of the United States, and "I mean to take Virginia at her word. I am under no constitutional obligations to a foreign country, which Virginia now claims to be."

Butler called the runaways "contraband of war" and refused to return them. In August Congress agreed and declared that all property taken from the enemy, including slaves, could be kept as spoils of war. But what would be done with the former slaves? Should they be put to work or given uniforms and guns and turned into soldiers?

Union general Thomas W. Sherman, who was stationed with his troops in Beaufort, South Carolina, asked for volunteers to help with the freed slaves. Governor John Andrew of Massachusetts arranged for Harriet Tubman to join a group of more than fifty doctors, teachers, ministers, and others headed south to help the Union cause.

It wasn't clear to Tubman what her role would be with the Union army. At first she thought she was going to spy for them. "They changed the program," she said many years later. Instead of spying they wanted her to distribute clothes to the slaves who were crossing the lines to the Union side. But the program for her would change often. Harriet Tubman would find many ways to serve the Union army.

Chapter Eleven

SPY, GUIDE, LAUNDRESS, AND NURSE

The good Lord has come down
to deliver my people,
and I must go and help Him.
—Harriet Tubman, on her work with the Union army

A Union soldier

"THEY WOULDN'T LET no colored people go down south then," Tubman said later, "unless they went with some of the officers as a servant; so they got a gentleman from New York to take me as a servant. He was stopping at a big hotel on Broadway and I went to the parlor and they sent for him and he came down." She took an instant dislike to his "strutting about," and he seemed to feel the same about her. She refused to go with him, and instead traveled alone.

She went to the once-beautiful city of Beaufort, South Carolina. It was a shambles, having been looted and destroyed by Union soldiers. The whites of the city were gone. They left everything behind, including their slaves, who were dressed in whatever they could find: cast-off uniforms, blankets, pieces of

A Confederate soldier

Reaction to President Lincoln's Emancipation Proclamationas reported in:

Douglass' Monthly

ROCHESTER, NEW YORK, FEBRUARY 1863

The news of the President's great act was received with a thrill throughout the loyal North. Among men who love liberty, the rejoicings were universal. Extra newspapers were eagerly bought in the great cities, and men stopped in the streets to read the decree. The general joy was augmented by the simultaneous intelligence of the victories in Tennessee and Mississippi. Altogether, the New Year began with a general burst of enthusiasm. May the year establish Liberty, and crown it with Peace. In New York, several congratulatory meetings have been held...On Monday evening the "Sons of Freedom," an association of colored people, held a public celebration in Cooper Institute; the great hall was crowded to suffocation...Rev. H.H. Garnet presided with dignity, reading the Proclamation, and making a most appropriate and eloquent address. Having finished the reading of the Proclamation, he said 'My friends, we must remember that it is God who has brought about this great event. Let us, first of all, rise to our feet, and stand in solemn reverence and thankfulness before him.' The whole assembly rose. 'Now, then,' said Mr. Garnet, 'let us give three cheers for the President of the United States...The whole proceedings were very interesting, exciting, and impressive...In Boston, on New Year's day appropriate exercises were held in anticipation of the Proclamation. A jubilee concert was given in the afternoon at which Josiah Quincy, Jr., presided and made a speech, and Ralph Waldo Emerson read an original poem...At Tremont Temple a meeting was held, continuing through the day and evening... In the evening when the Proclamation came to hand, Charles W. Slack read it to the audience, who received it with uproarious applause, shouting, tossing up their hats, rapping on the floor with their canes, and singing "Blow ye the trumpet, blow."... At Washington, a great flock of contraband— men, women and children—assembled at the headquarters of Superintendent Nichols, and engaged in a variety of congratulatory exercises. They sang the 'Negro Boatman's Song' with a volume of voice that could be heard miles… In addition to the above, many other demonstrations were made, in various Northern cities, of which we have no room here to make chronicle; nor have we space for mentioning any of the innumerable references to the Great Event which were made in the Churches on the first Sunday of the year. The only regret which mingles with the general joy is for the omissions which the President thought prudent to make. But the conviction already prevails, that, if Providence shall now give victories to our arms, the entire system of American Slavery will be speedily extinct— cleansed like a stain from the face of the land! God hasten the hour!—*N.Y. Independent.*

TO-DAY—this first day of January, 1863—thanks to Abraham Lincoln, President of these United States—millions of our fellow-beings, hitherto in chains, can stand up FREE. Such a new year, such a "happy new year," has never dawned upon them before…

EFFECT OF THE PROCLAMATION— Gen. Clusseret has written to a Senator, under date of Winchester, January 7, a letter, in which he says: "We have received—Gen. Milroy and myself—the President's Proclamation of Freedom. Inconsequence, we yesterday posted on the walls of Winchester, and scattered throughout the country, from farm to farm, an order from Gen. Milroy notifying all slaves that they are free, beginning from the 1st of January, and have the right to claim wages from their masters, or quit them, and that in this case, the troops will protect their rights precisely as they will those of all other citizens." A correspondent of the *New York Tribune* also writes of the effect the proclamation has already produced: —"The northern neck of Virginia, the heart of aristocratic and wealthy slavery, is alive with avast hegira of bondmen and bond women, traveling under President Lincoln's pass. The proclamation is depopulating the whole region between the Rappahannock and the Potomac. In farm wagons, in coaches, on horseback, afoot and in buggies, with valuable property, in every case, this second movement from Egypt to the promised land fills the highways and the woods…

carpet, and potato sacks. Harriet Tubman put former slaves to work at the Christian Commission House giving out clothes, food, and books to the Union soldiers. Then with some money from the government she set up a washhouse where her workers washed and sewed soldiers' clothes and baked bread and cake. For many of them this was the first time they were getting paid for their work.

Many former slaves had traveled a long way to reach safety behind Union lines. They arrived hungry and with no decent clothing. "Most of them," Tubman dictated in a letter to Franklin B. Sanborn of Massachusetts, "are very destitute, almost naked. I am trying to find places for those able to work, and provide for them as best I can, so as to lighten the burden on the government as much as possible, while at the same time they learn to respect themselves by earning their own living."

During the day she worked in the army hospital bathing and nursing patients suffering from malaria, smallpox, dysentery, and other diseases. Tubman had faith that God would protect her from infection until it was her time. When it did come, she declared, she was "ready to go."

Each night she baked huge loaves of gingerbread and about fifty pies, and prepared two casks of root beer. Then, in the morning, she paid former slaves to sell the cakes and drinks to the soldiers. She was working hard, not only to support herself but so she could send money home to her family in Auburn.

Soon after arriving in Beaufort, she met General David Hunter, a dedicated enemy of slavery. Hunter recruited African Americans into the Union ranks. They were not "fugitive slaves," he wrote to members of Congress in defense of his policies. "It is the masters who have in every instance been the 'fugitives'—running away from loyal slaves as well as loyal soldiers." He called the former slaveholders "fugitive rebels."

Hunter had made his own "Emancipation Proclamation" many months before President Lincoln announced his. In May 1862 Hunter declared all slaves in the districts under his command to be free. This included all of South Carolina, Georgia, and Florida. Almost one year earlier, in August 1861, Union general John C. Fremont, in charge of Union forces in Missouri, had made the same proclamation in that state. Lincoln voided both orders.

General John Fremont

However, on September 22, 1862, Lincoln declared that as of January 1, 1863, the more than three million slaves in the Confederate states would be free. Of course, for the slaves to be truly free, the Confederacy would have to be defeated. With Lincoln's Emancipation Proclamation the Civil War became a fight both to save the Union and to free the slaves.

At noon on January 1, 1863, Secretary of State Seward brought the proclamation to Lincoln and, according to a report in the New York newspaper *The Rochester Express*, "Mr. Lincoln took a pen, dipped it in ink, moved his hand to the place for the signature, held it a moment, and then removed his hand and dropped the pen.... 'I've been shaking hands since nine o'clock this morning,' he said. 'My right arm is almost paralyzed.' He knew this was a pivotal moment, and said, 'If my name ever goes down in history it will be for this act, and my whole soul is in it.' He then took the pen and signed his name, looked up, and said, 'That will do.'"

People in the South were outraged. An editorial in *The Richmond Whig* called Lincoln an "enraged tyrant."

General David Hunter

Escaped slaves serving officers in the Union army, Fort Monroe, 1861

The Richmond Enquirer declared it was his intention to incite a slave rebellion.

On New Year's Day abolitionists gathered in churches and in the streets to celebrate. "God Almighty's New Year will make the United States the land of freedom!" declared one African-American minister.

In Beaufort there was a huge three-hour celebration with soldiers and former slaves. Someone asked Harriet Tubman why she didn't join the party. "I had my jubilee three years ago," she said. "I rejoiced all I could then; I can't rejoice no more."

She had dreamed of emancipation in the spring of 1861 at the New York home of Reverend Garnet. She had rejoiced then.

Perhaps there was another reason for her low spirits. Lincoln's proclamation promised freedom only to the slaves in the states in rebellion. It left out those in the slaves states, including Maryland, that did not join the Confederacy. Whatever family and friends she had there had been excluded from the terms of the proclamation.

While others celebrated until well past nightfall, Tubman returned to her cabin to bake and prepare root beer for the next day.

≈

In May 1863 General Hunter asked Tubman to join troops taking several gunboats on a raid up the Combahee River. The mission was to remove mines left in the water by Confederate soldiers and to cut off enemy supply lines by destroying railroads and bridges. At Tubman's recommendation, General Hunter named Colonel James Montgomery to be the commander of the expedition. Montgomery was one of John Brown's men who had escaped capture at Harper's Ferry.

The gunboats passed plantations as they traveled along the river. Slaves heard these were Lincoln's boats and rushed to the riverbank to be taken aboard and set free.

"I never seen such a sight," Tubman said later. "Here you'd see a woman with a pail on her head, rice a-smoking in it just as she'd taken it from the fire, young one hanging on behind, one hand round her forehead to hold on . . . on her dress two or three more . . . one woman brought two pigs, a white one and a black one; we took them all on board; named the white pig Beauregard, and the black pig Jeff Davis." The white one was named after the Confederate general who had captured Fort Sumter and the black one was named after the president of the Confederacy.

"Moses," Colonel Montgomery shouted over the ruckus, "you'll have to give them a song."

And Harriet Tubman sang:

in due time ~~at the next session of congress~~
And the executive will recommend that

all citizens of the United States who shall have
remained loyal thereto throughout the rebellion, shall (upon the restoration of the constitutional relation between the United States, and
their respective states, and people, if that relation
shall have been suspended or disturbed) be
compensated for all losses by acts of the United
States, including the loss of slaves.--
    In witness whereof, I have
L. S.   hereunto set my hand, and caused.
    the seal of the United States to be
    affixed
    Done at the City of Washington,
    this twenty second day of September,
in the year of our Lord, one thousand, eight
hundred and sixty two, and sixty two,
and of the Independence of the United
States, the eighty seventh.
                        Abraham Lincoln.
By the President.
    William H Seward,
        Secretary of State

*Facsimile of a portion of President Lincoln's draft of the Preliminary Proclamation of Emancipation,
September 1862, from the original in the Library of the State of New York, Albany*

Come from the east
Come from the west
Among all the glorious nations
This glorious one's the best.
Come along; come along; don't be alarmed,
For Uncle Sam is rich enough
To give you all a farm.

After each verse of her song the former slaves threw up their hands and shouted, "Glory!"

For the Union, it was a glorious expedition. Its soldiers chased the enemy from their posts along the river. They confiscated food and animals and disrupted Confederate supply lines.

When they returned to camp, Tubman was kept busy helping to provide for the more than seven hundred and fifty newly freed slaves who had come back with her and joined their camp. They had to be fed, clothed, and given places to live.

Tubman was often sent to spy behind enemy lines, to bring back information on the number of soldiers and artillery. She was sometimes caught in the middle of a battle with bullets flying past, but she had great faith and never seemed to be afraid.

Chapter Twelve

HORRORS OF WAR

And now a word of this woman
—this black heroine—
in patriotism, sagacity, energy, ability,
and all that elevates human character,
she is head and shoulders above...many
who vaunt their patriotism.
—From a June 1863 article on Harriet Tubman in
the *Wisconsin State Journal*

HARRIET TUBMAN WAS at the disastrous 1863 battle in
Charleston Harbor.

"We saw the lightning, and that was the guns, and then
we heard the thunder, and that was the big guns," Tubman
said of the attacks in July through September 1863 on Fort
Wagner, a Confederate stronghold. "Then we heard the rain
falling, and that was the drops of blood falling; and when we
came to get the crops, it was the dead that we reaped."

"Men lying in every possible attitude," said an eyewitness,
"their limbs bent into unnatural shapes."

Among the Union soldiers in the assault were those in the
Fifty-fourth Massachusetts, an African-American regiment
under the command of Colonel Robert Gould Shaw, the son
of prominent white abolitionists. He was twenty-five, married

African-American Union soldiers, 1861

just two months, and so sure he would fall in the assault that he gave a pack of letters and personal papers to a reporter for safe-keeping. Tubman said later that she had fed him his last meal.

Shaw led the charge and was one of the first killed, riddled with seven bullets. In an effort to dishonor him, Confederates threw his body into an open grave and covered it with twenty dead black soldiers. Shaw's family refused suggestions that he be moved to a private grave. They expressed great pride that he had been buried with his men.

It was a bloody battle. About one-third of the Fifty-fourth was lost. In all, more than fifteen hundred Union soldiers were

*Colonel
Robert Gould Shaw*

Nurse Clara Barton

injured, killed, missing, or captured, against fewer than two hundred Confederate casualties.

The injured white soldiers were sent to nearby Hilton Head and put under the care of nurse Clara Barton. The African-American soldiers were sent to Beaufort and were cared for by Harriet Tubman.

"I would go to the hospital, I would, early every morning," Tubman said of her work in Beaufort. "I'd get a big chunk of ice, I would, and put it in a basin, and fill it with water; then I'd take a sponge and begin. First man I'd come to, I'd thrash away the flies, and they'd rise, they would, like bees around a hive. Then I'd begin to bathe their wounds, and by the time I'd bathed off three or four, the fire would have melted the ice and made the water warm, and it would be as red as clear blood. Then I'd go and get more ice, I would, and by the time I got to the next ones, the flies would be round the first ones black and thick as ever."

The fighting continued for almost two months, until September 7, when Confederate forces abandoned Fort Wagner. Later, when Sergeant William H. Carney was awarded the Medal of Honor for his bravery in the Fort Wagner battles, the first African American to receive the award, he said, "I only did my duty."

From the very beginning of the war Harriet Tubman talked of enlisting African Americans. Whenever it was done it was considered "an experiment." But it was an experiment that began in the South.

In April 1861, shortly after the firing on Fort Sumter, an African-American Confederate troop was recruited in Tennessee. In 1862 there was a Louisiana regiment of more than a thousand free blacks. Union major Christian A. Fleetwood said of the Fourth U.S. Colored Troops, "There is no telling what the result of the war might have been had the South kept up the policy of enlisting the freemen and emancipating the slaves and their families." But the early victories convinced the Confederacy it could win the war without them. By 1865, when the tide had clearly turned against the South, General Lee was authorized to recruit two hundred thousand African Americans, but by then it was too late.

Beginning in May 1863, African Americans were enlisted directly into the Union army. Their units were in 449 battles. Union brigadier general Daniel Ullman, a white man, said of them, "They are far more earnest than we. I have talked with hundreds of them." They knew they had a real stake in the outcome of the war. "If we are unsuccessful they will be remanded to a worse slavery than before…if they are taken, they will be tortured and hung." Ullman described his black troops as "daring and desperate fighters."

Harriet Tubman was a soldier of a different kind. She worked behind the lines and she worked nonstop. After more than two years at the front, she was exhausted. She missed her family, and sometime in the fall of 1863 she returned to Auburn, New York. In November she visited Saint Catharines, in Canada. By early 1864 she was back in South Carolina, and then she accompanied Colonel James Montgomery's regiment to Fernandina, Florida. She worked there as a cook, laundress, and nurse.

Many soldiers at the Union camp in Fernandina were suffering from dysentery, a painful intestinal ailment. "They was dying off like sheep," Tubman said. Even the doctor in charge was suffering. "I dug some roots and herbs and made a tea for the doctor, and the disease stopped on him. And then he said, 'Give it to the soldiers.'" She made a huge supply of her herbal remedy, and the general had a soldier "give it to all in the camp that needed it, and it cured them."

The war was taking a toll on Tubman. She was once again suffering from the injury she sustained when the two-pound weight hit her head many years earlier. In June 1864 she went back to Auburn to visit her family and to rest. In August she went to Boston. While there she met the famous black anti-slavery activist Sojourner Truth. Both women had been born slaves. Both were deeply religious. Truth was on her way to Washington, D.C., to meet with President Lincoln, and invited Tubman to accompany her.

Harriet Tubman declined.

"I didn't like Lincoln in them days," she said later. "You see, we colored people didn't understand then he was our friend." She only knew that African-American soldiers were paid half of what white soldiers got. "We didn't like that."

In the spring of 1865 she prepared to return to South Carolina. By then the war was almost over.

Two battles in July 1863, at Gettysburg, Pennsylvania, and Vicksburg, Mississippi, had marked the turning point in the war. The Union victory at Gettysburg, the bloodiest battle of the war, with more than forty thousand left dead or wounded, sent the Confederate commander, General Robert E. Lee, and his troops back south in retreat. The Union's victory at Vicksburg gave it control of the Mississippi River, effectively splitting the Confederacy in two and stopping the easy movement of Rebel solders and supplies.

On Sunday morning, April 2, 1865, Jefferson Davis, the president of the Confederacy, was in his pew in Richmond's St. Paul's Church. A soldier brought him a telegram from Lee: "Richmond must be evacuated this evening."

The news traveled quickly.

Davis and his Cabinet met. They packed up their records and hurried out of the city. Many others left, too. But many more could not get out. They took whatever they could carry and gathered in the center of the city.

Rebel soldiers burned bridges, boats in the James River, cotton and tobacco warehouses, and arsenals. They were ordered to leave nothing of strategic value for the conquering Union army. Banks were set on fire. Railroad depots were torched. Hundreds of barrels of liquor were rolled into the streets and smashed. Whiskey flowed through the gutters, fumes filling the air. Houses were burned. Looters stole the rest—furniture, clothing, food, and jewelry. According to one newspaper report, retreating Confederate soldiers found some liquor and "from that moment law and order ceased to exist; chaos came, and pandemonium reigned."

Union forces attacking Confederate soliders with hand grenades at the Battle of Vicksurg, July 1863

At last the Union troops took control of the city, and on Tuesday, April 4, President Lincoln visited Richmond. He was quickly surrounded by thousands of African Americans who called him "Father" and "Master Abraham."

"Glorious news! Richmond has been taken," Union Quartermaster Sergeant John C. Brock wrote in a letter. "That city, which has been striving for so long, and which has been the cause of so much toil and anguish, and bloodshed, has at last fallen!"

The Battle at Gettysburg from the Confederate side

A Letter to
The Christian Recorder
An African-American Newspaper
APRIL 15, 1865

For the Christian Recorder.

FROM CAMP WM. PENN.

Chelton Hills, Pa., April 6th, 1865.

Mr. Editor: —I beg your indulgence for intruding upon your columns so soon again. As there are so many very interesting incidents occurring, just about this time, in and around Camp Wm. Penn, we think it would be interesting to so many of our brave colored soldiers, who have left this camp and are now on the field of battle, or doing garrison duty in the South, to hear from us through your paper.

On last Saturday evening we had a very entertaining homespun lecture, from a colored woman, known as **Harriet Tubman**. It was the first time we had the pleasure of hearing her. She seems to be very well known by the community at large, as the great Underground Rail Road woman, and has done a good part to many of her fellow creatures, in that direction. During her lecture, which she gave in her own language, she elicited considerable applause from the soldiers of the 24th regiment, U.S.C.T., now at the camp. She gave a thrilling account of her trials in the South, during the past three years, among the contrabands and colored soldiers, and how she had administered to thousands of them, and cared for their numerous necessities. After the lecture, resolutions were passed by the regiment to be published in the *Recorder*. The lecture was interspersed with several gems of music. Professors Burris and Turner presided at the organ. After a liberal collection for the lecturer, the meeting adjourned....A.B.

The delight of the people, Brock wrote, "can neither be expressed nor described. Old men and women tottering on their canes, would make their way to a Union soldier, catch him by the hand, and exclaim, 'Thank God, honey, that I have

General Ulysses S. Grant

General Robert E. Lee

lived to see this day! I have been looking, and longing, and praying for you to come; and thank God, He has heard our prayers, and preserved our lives to see this salvation!'"

Army chaplain Garland H. White, an African American, was among the first Union soldiers to enter Richmond. The officers and men of his regiment called upon him to make a speech. "Of course, I readily complied," White wrote in a letter several days later, "and proclaimed for the first time in that city freedom to all."

White also wrote of the scene in Richmond.

"There were parents looking up children who had been sold south." Among them was an old woman looking for her son who had been sold when he was a small boy to a lawyer named Richard Toombs of Georgia. The woman had seen Toombs in Richmond with rebel troops and asked about her child. "He ran off from me at Washington," she was told. "I have since learned he is living somewhere in the state of Ohio."

Chaplain Garland H. White was from Ohio, so he was brought to the woman and her friend. They asked White a series of questions. Then there was a tearful reunion. The friend told him, "This is your mother, Garland."

White later wrote, "I cannot express the joy I felt, at this happy meeting…God is on the side of the righteous."

On April 9, at a farmhouse at Appomattox, Virginia, Confederate general Robert E. Lee surrendered to Union general Ulysses S. Grant.

Lee's soldiers surrounded him after the surrender. They praised his valor, and tears came to his eyes. "We

fought through the war together," he said. "I have done the best I could for you. My heart is too full to say more."

When news of the surrender reached Union troops they fired their guns to celebrate. Grant ordered it to stop. "The war is over," he said, "and it is ill-becoming to rejoice in the downfall of a gallant foe."

With the end of the war, for the first time in her life Harriet Tubman was truly free. She was no longer a runaway. She could not be arrested and returned to slavery.

"How many thousands have been wounded and slain, in striving to obtain this prize," Sergeant Brock wrote in his letter. "How many wives have been made widows! How many mothers have mourned the loss of favorite sons! How many orphans have wept the loss of beloved fathers!"

It is estimated that there were more than six hundred thousand casualties in the Civil War.

In the South people had been dispersed. Because their Confederate money was now worthless, many were penniless.

Their stores and barns were empty. More than half of Southern livestock had been killed. Farms were left bare and barren. Many once-elegant Southern mansions were now just piles of burned stones. Riverways were blocked; docks, harbors, and railroads had been destroyed.

The war had preserved the Union, but it had broken the nation.

Chapter Thirteen

Ghosts, Cows, and Buried Treasure

You wouldn't think that after
I served the flag so faithfully
I should come to want under its folds.
—Harriet Tubman, 1907

The crowd gathered at Fort Sumter, April 14, 1865

AT THE TIME of the surrender, Harriet Tubman was working as a nurse for injured black soldiers. She was at Fort Monroe in Hampton, Virginia, a little more than one hundred miles from Appomattox.

On Friday, April 14, five days after the surrender, the same U.S. flag that had been lowered at Fort Sumter four years earlier was raised there in celebration. The flag was frayed and torn, but that did not seem to dampen spirit. People cheered. Cannons on boats in the harbor were fired to salute the flag.

That morning General Grant was

in Washington attending a meeting of Lincoln's cabinet. Arrangements were made for Grant to accompany the president to Ford's Theatre that night to see a performance of the comedy, *Our American Cousin*. But Grant was called away. Instead, President Lincoln went to the theater with his wife and two guests.

Lincoln sat in a high-backed chair in a private balcony. Just past ten o'clock, near the end of the show, John Wilkes Booth, a half-crazed actor and supporter of the Confederacy, entered the president's private box. He had a small gun in one hand and a knife in the other. Booth shot the president. Someone grabbed him, but he broke loose and shouted, "*Sic semper tyrannis!*" (Thus always to tyrants), the motto on the state seal of Virginia. Booth was pursued and finally cornered twelve days later in a barn near Bowling Green, Virginia. When he refused to surrender, he was shot and killed.

Lincoln was taken to a house near the theater. Gideon Welles, a member of the president's cabinet, was at his side. "The night was dark and cloudy," Welles wrote in his diary. He stayed with the president through the night. Early the next morning he left and took a short walk. People had gathered outside. "Intense grief was on every countenance," Welles wrote, especially the African Americans.

John Wilkes Booth running off after shooting President Lincoln

"There were at this time more of them," waiting nearby for news "than of whites."

President Lincoln died at 7:22 A.M., April 15, 1865.

Harriet Tubman was stunned.

The assassination of the president was part of a larger conspiracy. The same night that Lincoln was shot, Booth's accomplice Lewis Payne entered the bedroom of Tubman's friend Secretary of State William Seward. The secretary was slowly recovering from injuries from a fall from his horse-drawn carriage. Payne stabbed Seward several times. He also seriously injured Seward's son Frederick. Both men survived.

Tubman visited Seward in his Washington sickbed. While she was there, she told him of "dreadful abuses" at the hospital for African-American soldiers at Fort Monroe, where the injured died at a rate more than double that of white soldiers. She also complained to Seward that she had not been paid for her years of service to the Union cause.

Seward loaned her twelve dollars, to be added to the money she still owed him for the house and farm he had sold to her.

In response to the problems at the hospital, Seward sent her to the surgeon general, Dr. Joseph K. Barnes. Barnes appointed her "Nurse or Matron at the colored hospital." He hoped that with a title she would command enough respect to effect changes. But when she reported back to the hospital she was not made a nurse or matron, as promised, so she left.

Seward wrote to General David Hunter to get Tubman pay for her service to the army, but with no hope of getting paid anytime soon, she went home to Auburn. She needed to support her parents and earn enough money to repay her debt to Secretary Seward.

The war was over. The South and slavery had been defeated on the battlefield. The official end to slavery in the

United States came in December 1865, eight months after the surrender at Appomattox. At the end of January 1865 Congress passed the Thirteenth Amendment, which made having a slave illegal. By December three-quarters of the states had ratified the amendment, making it law. That marked the official end to slavery in the United States.

Former slaves now had their freedom, but many had little else. They had no jobs, no food, and no homes. They also suffered in other ways. While slavery had been outlawed, unfair treatment of African Americans continued. Harriet Tubman experienced it in October 1865 on her way home to Auburn.

She boarded a train in Philadelphia and showed the conductor her army-issued half-fare ticket. "Come, hustle out of here!" he shouted. Because she was an African American he demanded she sit in the smoking car. He grabbed her but she held on to her seat. The conductor called two other men to help. They pried her fingers from her seat, wrenching her arm in the struggle, and threw her into the baggage car.

Tubman called the conductor a "copperhead scoundrel," and he grabbed her by the neck. She shouted that she was as "proud of being a black woman as you are of being white."

She got off the train in New York City and stayed there with friends who took care of her while she recovered from the beating. Nothing came of plans to sue the railroad. When she was able, Tubman returned to Auburn, but as a result of her injuries on the train she couldn't work.

While in Auburn her parents lived with her. Through the winter of 1865–66, with no money and no work, she had to take down the fences around her property and burn them in her fireplace to keep warm. She survived the winter with the help of her abolitionist white friends, the same people who had assisted her before the war.

With money scarce, Tubman's mother had to do without two of her greatest loves—tea and tobacco. She was inconsolable, yelling and cursing at her daughter. One day, when Tubman could no longer take the abuse, she hid in a closet. When she came out, she called to her sister-in-law Catherine Stewart, who was living with her.

"Put on the soup pot," she told her. "Not the little one, the big one."

Stewart told Tubman she could put the pot on, but she had nothing to put in it. Tubman told her not to worry. She had plans to fill it.

She took her shopping basket and started toward the stores in downtown Auburn. It was late. The shopkeepers were getting ready to close up and go home. They gave her their left-over vegetables, meat, and soup bones, some as a gift and some with a promise that she would pay when she could.

There was food that night for her and all the people staying with her, but the next day the pot was empty again. Feeding everyone was a constant struggle.

It was a large household. Along with her elderly parents, her niece Kessiah Bawley, husband John and their seven children, stayed with Tubman, as did her brother John Stewart, who had severe rheumatism. She also took in boarders.

One of her boarders was Sarah Parker, an elderly blind widow. Another was Nelson Davis, a former slave and army veteran. He was a tall, handsome man, but he was sickly. He suffered from tuberculosis. At about the time he moved in, Tubman learned that her first husband, John Tubman, had met a violent end. On Monday morning September 30, 1867, he and his white neighbor Robert Vincent had an argument.

Vincent threatened Tubman with an axe. Tubman ran off. That evening they met again by chance, and this time Vincent took out a pistol and shot Tubman, who fell to the ground. According to a local newspaper, the cold-hearted Vincent just walked away.

Vincent was arrested and charged with murder. At his trial he claimed self-defense, that he was on his way home when Tubman "rushed out of the woods with a club." Tubman's thirteen-year-old son, Thomas, had witnessed the shooting, and testified that his father had not attacked Vincent. After just ten minutes of deliberation the all-white jury declared Robert Vincent not guilty. That was the expected outcome. Even in 1867, with slavery ended, there was little justice in many places for African Americans.

On Thursday, March 18, 1869, Harriet Tubman married the much younger Davis. They became partners in Tubman's businesses and works of charity. In 1874 they adopted a daughter, Gertie. Little is known about Gertie, only that in 1900 she married a man named Watson.

Tubman and Davis set up a brick-making business at one end of her property. She also worked as a housekeeper for some of her wealthier neighbors.

Tubman and Davis joined the AME Zion Church of Auburn. During services she always sat near the front, bent forward. At times she stood and others joined her as she shouted and sang her praises of God. Religion directed her life, and even though she never learned to read or write, she often quoted the Bible.

In 1868 Sara H. Bradford wrote a biography of Harriet Tubman. Many people question the accuracy of the book. It and later editions are the sources of the probably inflated numbers of Tubman's nineteen trips to Maryland beginning in 1850 and the three hundred slaves she rescued. Its publication was a work of charity. Bradford took no profits from the sale of the books. They all went to Tubman for her and her good works.

Tubman also raised money with Freedmen's Fairs. People sewed aprons, bags, pin cushions, rag dolls, towels, and other items to be sold at the fairs. They sold home-baked cookies and cakes, used clothes, and copies of the Bradford biography. At the 1868 fair more than five hundred dollars was raised for the poor. The next year she organized a fair to benefit needy people in South Carolina.

Surely it was Harriet Tubman's desire to help so many people, as well as her need for money to support herself and her family, that got her involved in a swindle.

In October 1873 two African-American men, John Thomas and Stevenson, who was also known as Johnson, came to the area with a story about a hidden trunk filled with Confederate gold coins worth about five thousand dollars. They said the coins could be seized in South Carolina as money belonging to the state. That's why they brought it to Auburn and were willing to sell it all for just two thousand dollars. They told their story to Tubman's brother John Stewart. Stewart told the men he didn't have the money to buy the gold but perhaps his sister could raise it from her wealthy friends.

When the con men met Tubman they gained her trust by mentioning the name of a black minister who had moved from the area. They also spoke of Alfred Bowley, Tubman's nephew. She believed the men and was convinced that this was her chance to solve her money troubles.

She spoke with Anthony Shimer, a local businessman, who gave her the two thousand dollars. She went with Stevenson to meet Harris, who Tubman believed was a former slave. He was the man with the gold. Then she followed the two men across several fields, over a few fences, and into a forest until they came to a pile of wooden rails. The men lifted the rails, dug in a pile of leaves, and at last pulled out a large box about three feet long. It was wrapped in canvas.

The men then demanded the two thousand dollars, but Tubman refused to give it to them. First, she insisted, she must see the gold. The men began a futile, phony search for the key to the box. Neither of the men had the key, so they went off to get it. They left Harriet Tubman in the woods with the money and the box.

She inspected the box. It didn't even have a keyhole! She realized the men's story about needing a key to open it had been a lie. She had been tricked.

Tubman looked around. It was dark in the forest, and frightening. She thought about the many scary stories she had heard about moonlit nights and buried treasures. She started out of the woods, but then stopped. She saw something big and white. Was it a ghost? She slowly moved closer. To her great relief she saw it was a cow. But the animal was startled by Tubman and started to run. There were other cows in the woods and they ran, too, starting a small stampede.

In the midst of the cows and confusion, the two swindlers returned.

Tubman didn't remember what happened next, just that when she woke up she was still in the woods, only now she was tied up and gagged. All of Shimer's money had been stolen.

Her brother John Stewart, Shimer, and a third man found Harriet cut and dazed. They found and opened the box that the swindler claimed held Confederate gold. It was filled with rocks.

When news of the swindle was reported in local newspapers, Tubman's neighbors sympathized with her. Her charitable nature convinced most people of her complete innocence in the affair. The biggest loser in the whole misadventure was Anthony Shimer. He had lost two thousand dollars.

Chapter Fourteen

DIFFICULT LAST YEARS

I am at peace with God and all mankind.
—Harriet Tubman, in 1913

THE 1870S AND 1880s were difficult decades for Harriet Tubman.

Her father had been stricken with rheumatism. In his final years he needed constant help and much of the burden of his care fell on Harriet. Benjamin Ross died in his mid-eighties, in 1871.

One year later Tubman's good friend and benefactor William Seward died. At his funeral, according to a newspaper report, "Just before the coffin was to be closed...a woman black as night stole quietly in, and laying a wreath of field flowers *on his feet*, as quietly glided out again." That woman was Harriet Tubman, paying final tribute to Seward.

During the 1870s, Tubman's mother, who had always

been a stubborn, argumentative woman, became even more difficult. Tubman was her primary caregiver and Green directed her many complaints at her. Harriet "Rit" Green died in 1880 at the age of approximately ninety-five.

Harriet Tubman's troubles continued.

Sometime in the early 1880s Tubman's house, along with almost all her personal possessions, was destroyed by fire. She and her husband, Nelson Davis, used bricks made on their property to build a new home. Their Auburn neighbors raised money to help pay for it.

She and Davis started a business raising hogs. They fed them food scraps and other refuse collected from their neighbors. In 1884 most of the animals mysteriously died. It was suspected that rat poison had seeped into the garbage they had been feeding the hogs.

Davis's tuberculosis worsened. He died in 1888. He was just forty-five years old.

In the late 1880s Tubman's brother William Henry Stewart came to live with her. In about 1890 Stewart's son John Isaac and his wife, Helena, had a daughter, but her birth was very difficult. While Helena lay dying, Harriet promised to raise the child. "Now I die happy," Helena Stewart said just before she passed away. Tubman was already an old woman, and now she was responsible for the care of an infant.

To help with her money troubles she petitioned for back pay for her years of service to the Union army, and at last, in 1895, she was granted a pension of eight dollars a month. However, the money was not for her service. It was paid to her as the widow of Davis, a disabled Civil War veteran. Finally, in 1889, more than twenty years after the end of the war, twelve dollars a month was added to her pension for her work as a nurse for the Union army.

President Andrew Johnson

This Ku Klux Klan warning appeared in a 1868 newspaper notice published in Alabama as a warning to people who supported the civil rights of African Americans.

Harriet Tubman wasn't the only one suffering. The years following the Civil War were difficult ones for the entire country.

What was to be done with the Southern states that had rebelled? President Andrew Johnson, who succeeded Lincoln, felt the states had no right to secede and were therefore never really out of the Union. He thought they should be easily allowed to regain their full rights. Most members of Congress disagreed. Their differences led to Johnson being accused of "high crimes and misdemeanors," and in 1868 there was an effort to remove him from office. He held on to the presidency by the narrowest of margins, just one vote.

The Fourteenth Amendment to the Constitution was ratified in 1868. It declared African Americans to be full citizens of the United States. The Fifteenth Amendment was ratified in 1870, guaranteeing them the right to vote. Nonetheless, they were subjected to discrimination. Surely when Harriet Tubman dreamed of freedom she envisioned African Americans having the same rights as whites, but she would never see an America with equal rights for blacks.

Many Southern state legislatures enacted "Black Codes," laws meant to restrict the freedoms of the newly freed slaves. And there were violent secret societies, including the Knights of the White Camellia, the White Brotherhood, the Pale Faces, and the most widely feared of them all, the Ku Klux Klan. The Klan was formed in 1868, and by the end of its first year it had five hundred thousand members. Within its first few years the Klan was guilty of committing thousands of murders of African Americans and of whites who defended the rights of blacks.

After the Civil War the history of the Underground Railroad and the courage of its stationmasters, agents, conductors, and brakemen was talked about openly. In 1872 William Still published his book *The Underground Rail Road: A Record of Facts, Authentic Narratives, Letters, etc, Narrating the Hardships, Hair-breadth Escapes, and Death Struggles of the Slaves in their Efforts for Freedom as Related by Themselves*

A lynching

Newspaper report from
The Christian Recorder
An African-American Newspaper
MARCH 3, 1881

PERSONAL. —**Harriet** Davis *nee* **Tubman**, better known as "Moses" of the rebellion, is endeavoring to establish a home for infirm colored people, in Auburn, N.Y. She served four years in the army acting as nurse, scout and spy, and made 16 trips to the South under the auspices of the Underground Railroad, paying her own expenses. General Saxon says: "She made many a raid inside the enemy's lines, displaying remarkable courage, zeal and fidelity." Such a woman ought certainly have the influence and support of the public in her undertaking.

and *Others, or Witnessed by the Author.* In it were almost eight hundred pages of firsthand accounts, records William Still had kept hidden to prevent runaway slaves and agents of the Railroad from being found out and arrested. With the book, Harriet Tubman's unselfish acts of bravery became even more widely known.

In 1886 Sarah Bradford issued a new, updated edition of her biography of Tubman. The book was read to England's Queen Victoria, who had an aide write to Tubman, "I read your book to Her Majesty, and she was pleased with it. She sends you this medal."

The round silver medal had on it a likeness of the Queen and members of her family. Tubman later said, "She also invited me to come over for her birthday party, but I didn't know enough to go."

Again, money from the sale of Bradford's book went to Tubman for her charitable works, which included feeding her many houseguests as well as other poor people, both blacks and whites. But Tubman felt she could do more. She dreamed of opening a home for needy African Americans.

In 1896 she bought a twenty-five-acre lot with a large building and several smaller buildings. She established a home for elderly black people and named it John Brown Hall. Several years later she gave the property to her church with the under-standing that it would remain a home for the needy.

Many of the women who supported Tubman's work to end slavery were also active in the women's suffrage move-ment, the fight to get women the right to vote. Tubman became active, too. She was a living example of the capabili-ties of women.

In 1888, at a meeting of the Auburn chapter of the Wom-en's Christian Temperance Union, she stood and said she had not come to teach them, but rather to learn and be taught. She spoke of all she did in the war as a scout, soldier, and nurse. She spoke of the brave women who stayed close to the battle lines to care for injured soldiers, and according to a report in a local newspaper, the *Auburn Morning Dispatch*, she asked, "If those deeds do not place woman as man's equal, what do?" She said God had helped her survive the war and God would even-tually grant women the right to vote.

In 1896 she spoke at a New York suffrage meeting. She was introduced to the audience by Susan B. Anthony, a leader of the movement, as "a faithful worker for the emancipation of her race." Her appearance at that convention was reported in "The Fight for the Ballot," an article in a local newspaper, the *Rochester Democrat and Chronicle*.

"The old woman was once a slave, and as she stood before the assemblage in her cheap black gown and coat and big black straw bonnet without adornment, her hand held in Miss Anthony's, she impressed one with the venerable dignity of her appearance." At first she spoke softly, but as she went on her voice rose. She talked of her personal history, her work as a slave, and her escape. She told how her master posted adver-tisements of a reward for her capture, and how she followed him and pulled the ads down. The newspaper reported that "many and many a slave was helped to Canada and freedom through her noble assistance."

In 1901 she was taken to a suffrage meeting in a church in Rochester. Susan B. Anthony and Elizabeth Cady Stanton were in the front of the room, and one of them called her to speak. People turned and there she was, fast asleep. She was almost eighty years old, and she still suffered the effects of the injury she suffered as a teenager.

Someone woke Tubman, and Susan B. Anthony announced, "I am glad to present to you Harriet Tubman, the 'conductor of the Underground Railroad.'"

"Yes, ladies," Tubman said. "I was the conductor of the Underground Railroad for eight years and I can say what most conductors can't say—I never ran my train off the track and I never lost a passenger." The audience applauded.

෨ఌ

The great courage Harriet Tubman had as a young woman didn't abandon her in her later years. In the 1890s she had an amazing experience in a Boston hospital.

The injury to her head did more than cause her to fall asleep at odd times during the day. Her head sometimes hurt so bad that it kept her up at night.

"When I was in Boston I walked out one day, I saw a great big building," she told her friend Samuel Hopkins. She was told the building was a hospital, so she walked in and asked a doctor, "Sir, do you think you could cut my head open?" She wouldn't let the doctors give her anything to limit the pain. Instead she bit a bullet and mumbled prayers during surgery, the same as she had seen soldiers do during the war. "He sawed open my skull, and raised it up," she told Hopkins, "and now it feels more comfortable."

When the operation was done she put on her bonnet and

started to walk home. But that was too much for her. She collapsed and was sent home in an ambulance.

Harriet Tubman continued to be active even into her eighties. In 1905 she was "for a woman of so great an age," according to an article in a Boston newspaper, "remarkably erect…her manner bright and her wit keen."

However, her housekeeping suffered. Perhaps it was just too difficult for her to keep things in order. Perhaps she had a slight case of dementia.

In 1906 Ellen Wright Garrison, the wife of William Lloyd Garrison II, came to visit Tubman. "We drove into her yard & such a leaking rummage heap as it was!" she wrote in a letter to her husband. "Quantities of old dry goods boxes for kindling, old cooking utensils sitting on the ground, old wagons & an old buggy in rags & tatters & dozens of other things & I counted five homely cats, four puppies & their dusty Ma, a dirty pig & lots of chickens besides 2 white children eating apples and looking very much at home." On a more positive note, Garrison also wrote, "Harriet came out of the kitchen looking quite well & brisk."

By 1910 her age had caught up to her. She could no longer walk, and needed a wheelchair. She moved into the home she had given to her church for the needy.

Tubman spent most of the winter of 1912–13 in bed. She was very thin and weak. She knew she was dying. During her last days many people came to her sickbed. She knew she would soon go on to the next world and told her visitors, "I go to prepare a place for you."

In death as in life she felt it was her role to do for others.

On March 10, 1913, she participated in a final religious service, which she directed. Her friends were there, including the Reverend Charles A. Smith and the Reverend E.U.A.

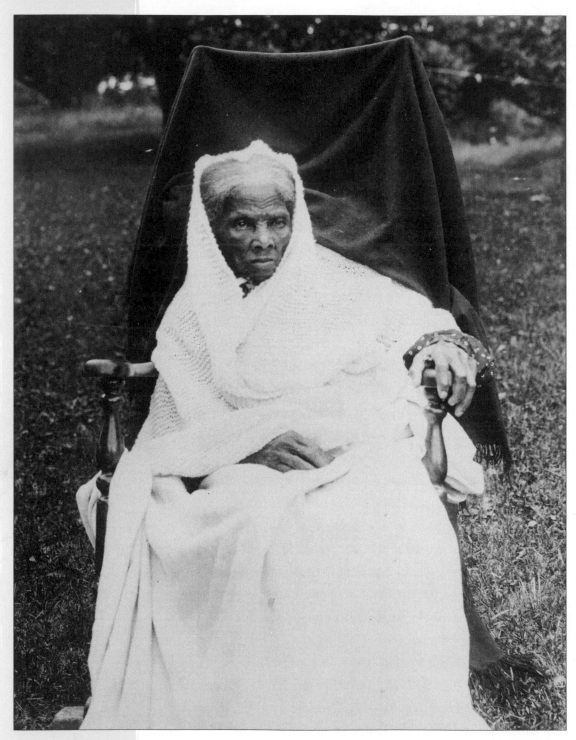

Harriet Tubman in 1911, at age 89

Brooks, and Eliza E. Peterson, who came from Texas to see her. According to the report in the local newspaper, *The Auburn Citizen*, "She joined in the singing when her cough did not prevent, and after receiving the sacrament she sank back in bed ready to die."

Harriet Tubman died that day of pneumonia at the age of ninety-one.

On March 13, the day of her funeral, hundreds of people paid their last respects to the woman known throughout Auburn as "Aunt Harriet." She was clothed in black with the medal sent to her by Queen Victoria pinned to her waist. In her hand was a crucifix. The top half of the casket was open. The lower half of the casket was draped with an American flag.

Tributes came from many of the people who had known and admired her.

John F. Jaeckel represented Auburn at the funeral. "No one of our fellow citizens," he said in his speech, "conferred greater distinction upon us than has she....The boys of my time always regarded her as a sort of supernatural being; our youthful imaginations were fired by the tales we had heard of her adventures and we stood in great awe of her....She was a woman of unusual judgment and great common sense."

Bishop G. L. Blackwell of Philadelphia said he wished there were a generation of women "as resolute as Aunt Harriet....Her sound mind, native ability, and sterling qualities placed her in the foremost rank of the best women of her race....The African Methodist Episcopal Zion Church feels honored for having had Aunt Harriet as a communicant in its ranks for many years."

"Something like this might I say of Araminta Ross...whose career was shaped by herself and her Lord," the journalist

Franklin B. Sanborn, one of the "Secret Six" who financially supported John Brown, wrote. He described "her general plan of life" as "to exist for the benefit of others, to whom she devoted magnificent powers, ever in readiness to serve the cause of humanity, as she understood it." She "could never see any fault in her friends; if money was given to her, she would give it away." He described her as "loyal to the death...with malice toward none, with charity for all."

Harriet Tubman was buried next to her brother William Henry and her niece and nephew Emma Stewart and William Henry Jr. Nearby was the grave of her husband Nelson Davis. She was buried with military honors. In her memory Mayor Charles W. Botster of Auburn called for all flags in the city to be flown at half-mast.

In June 1914 a bronze plaque in her memory was unveiled before a large audience in the Auburn Auditorium Theater. "This tablet will stand as a silent but effective monitor," former mayor E. Clarence Aiken told the many people who had come to the ceremony, "teaching the children of Auburn and of the state and of the country to lead such noble, unselfish, and helpful lives that they, too, may leave behind them memories which shall encourage others to live...Few memorials have been erected in this land to women...None has been erected to one who was at once a woman, a negro and a former slave...She was wise and unselfish."

The Reverend James E. Mason of Livingstone College, North Carolina, spoke, too. "We have met on many important occasions," he said of his association with Harriet Tubman, "in the cottages of the lowly and the palatial homes of the wealthy....Everywhere she was the same determined, generous, enthusiastic, race-loving, cheerful, heroic soul."

Later in the program Mayor Aiken introduced the evening's principal speaker, Dr. Booker T. Washington, one of the most influential African-American leaders of the time. He was a renowned educator and adviser to Presidents Theodore Roosevelt and William Howard Taft.

Despite Tubman's lack of any formal schooling, Washington declared her to be "one of the best educated persons who ever lived in this country." She was a woman educated by the harsh realities of her time. "It is most fitting," he said, "that the name of Harriet Tubman should be perpetuated by means of this tablet so that her memory and deeds can live in the minds and hearts of the present generation, and can be used as an object lesson for all time."

Important Dates *in the life of Harriet Tubman*

1822	Araminta Ross, later known as Harriet Tubman, is born in Dorchester County, Maryland. She is the slave of Edward Brodess. The year is not certain.
1828–35	Brodess hires out Tubman to various masters, beginning with James Cook and his wife, poor white farmers who live nearby.
1835	Tubman is seriously injured when hit on her forehead by a metal weight. The year is uncertain.
1836–42	Works for John Stewart.
1840	Her father, Ben Ross, gains his freedom by the terms of his owner, Anthony Thompson's, will.
1844	Marries John Tubman.
1849	Her slaveholder, Edward Brodess, dies, and fearful that she might be sold, she runs off.
1850	She makes the first of many trips south to lead slaves to freedom.
1851	Moves to St. Catharines, Canada. Returns to Dorchester County intent on leading her husband north. Instead she rescues several slaves.
1854	Rescues three of her brothers and several others, Christmas.
1856	Rescues Joe Bailey and a few others, November.
1857	Rescues her parents and takes them to Canada.
1858	Meets John Brown.
1859	Buys house and farm in Auburn, New York, from William Seward.
1860	Rescue of Charles Nalle in Troy, New York, April. In her last rescue mission, she leads seven slaves to freedom, December.
1861	Works for the Union army in South Carolina as a laundress and nurse.

1863	Leads the Union raid along the Combahee River, South Carolina.
1867	John Tubman, her estranged husband, dies.
1869	Marries Nelson Davis.
1871	Her father, Ben Ross, dies.
1873	Victimized in a buried-treasure swindle.
1874	She and Davis adopt a daughter, Gertie.
1880	Her mother, Harriet "Rit" Green, dies.
1888	Her husband, Nelson Davis, dies.
1896	Buys land on which to build a home for aged, sick, and homeless people.
1897	Awarded a medal by Queen Victoria of England.
1903	Donates the land she bought for a home for the aged to her church.
1908	The Harriet Tubman Home for Aged and Infirm Negroes opens.
1911	Moves into the home named for her.
1913	Dies of pneumonia on March 10.

A family portrait of Harriet Tubman taken in the 1900s

1863—President Lincoln signs the Emancipation Proclamation, January 1.

1865—Confederate general Lee surrenders to Union general Grant at Appomattox Court House, Virginia, April 9. Lincoln assassinated at Ford's Theatre, Washington, D.C., April 14.

Thirteenth Amendment to the Constitution is ratified, outlawing slavery, December.

1875—Congress passes Civil Rights Act guaranteeing equal rights on trains, in theaters, at inns, and on juries.

1878—An amendment is introduced in Congress to grant women the right to vote, but it doesn't pass until 1919. It's ratified and becomes law in 1920.

1896—In *Plessy vs. Ferguson* the Supreme Court rules that "separate but equal" facilities for whites and African Americans are lawful. This decision stands for more than fifty years.

Author's Note — *My Family's Civil War History*

My paternal great-grandfather Marcus Garfunkel (Baruch Mordecai) was the first of my ancestors to come here. He was born in Galicia, Austria, and moved to Goteborg, Sweden. Then he and his brother Moses meant to go to Australia but missed the boat, so instead, in 1856 they sailed to America. In August 1861 Uncle Moses married Masha Trager. Of my extended family, it's the Tragers who have the most interesting Civil War history.

Throughout the war years they lived in Columbia, South Carolina, where the road to secession began. Delegates met at a convention there in December 1860, but because of an outbreak of smallpox they moved to Charleston, where the actual vote to secede was taken. Columbia was left unscarred until 1865, when Union general William Tecumseh Sherman made his devastating sixty-mile-wide path of destruction from Atlanta to Savannah and then through South and North Carolina. His army burned railways, factories, homes, and bridges. They tore down telegraph lines, looted food supplies and private property, and seized tens of thousands of horses, mules, and cattle. In February 1865 Sherman's army entered Columbia and destroyed it. The Trager house was on a main street, but strangely it was left unharmed. Mrs. Trager spoke many languages, and the story told in Columbia was that she suspected one of the Union officers was a native of Germany so she spoke to him in German and begged him to spare her home. That story was told because the neighbors would surely have made the Tragers uncomfortable if they had known that it was the Tragers' Union connection that got them

special treatment. It's well documented that Mrs. Trager's brother Louis was a civilian scout and spy attached to Generals Grant and Halleck. In October 1863 he gave a detailed report of Confederate army units in several states. "Mr. Trager's account is full and no doubt reliable," Grant wrote to Halleck. He suggested Halleck meet with Trager. Trager was later captured and arrested, but by order of Confederate general Robert E. Lee he was later released. Apparently when the liberated Louis Trager heard where Sherman's army was headed, top Union generals got him special protection for his family.

In 1956 my dad took me from New York to visit his mother's family which by then had moved to Savannah, Georgia. "Whatever you do," Dad told me on the long train ride south, "don't mention General Sherman." And I didn't.

Ruins in Columbia,
South Carolina, 1865

Source Notes

In my research, the Bradford and Telford books based on interviews with Harriet Tubman were especially helpful. Both authors quoted her extensively, but in their efforts to capture her dialect they changed the spellings of simple words. "That" became "dat," "the" became "de," and "leave" became "lebe." I found the practice sometimes awkward and difficult to understand, and at all times patronizing. Here Tubman's words are recorded with proper spellings.

Along with the text I have included many period illustrations and excerpts from abolitionist newspapers. My hope is they will help the reader journey with me back to the nineteenth century, to the era of Harriet Tubman.

Preface

p. 1   "Do you like...I done it." Humez, p. 254. The interviewer for *The New York Herald* was Frank C. Drake, the husband of Emily Hopkins Drake, the niece of Sarah Bradford, Tubman's biographer.

p. 1   "The midnight...your works." Bradford, pp. 70–71.

Chapter One

p. 3   "The sad effects...without a dime reward." Bradford, p. 27.

p. 3   "Now, Joe...a licking." Bradford, p. 22.

p. 3   "Haven't I...against me?" Ibid, p. 23.

p. 3-4 "You belong to...take it." Ibid, p. 23.

p. 4   "This is...the last." Ibid, p. 23.

p. 4   "Next time...me know." Ibid, p. 23.

p. 4   "Keep going...keep going." Clinton, p. 221.

p. 4   "Go on or die." Humez, p. 236.

p. 4   "I never...a passenger." Larson, p. 276.

p. 4-5 On her death certificate, 1815 was listed as the year of Tubman's birth.

p. 5   "I never met...impudent curiosity." Douglass, p. 1.

p. 6   Despite the law, between 1808 and 1860 an estimated two hundred and fifty thousand blacks were illegally brought here from Africa.

p. 7   "What do...the boy?" Blassingame, p. 415, from an 1863 interview with Henry Stewart, Harriet Tubman's brother.

p. 7   "The first man...head open." Ibid.

Chapter Two

p. 9   "I grew . . . weed." Clinton p. 16

p. 9-10 "I never ate...before them." Ibid.

p. 10   "If I could...laid it on." Ibid.

p. 11   "Got into...rawhide down." Ibid, p. 18.

p. 11   "I was so . . . afraid of her." Humez, p.208

p. 12   "My hair...on my hair." Telford, p. 5.

p. 12   "That was the...I couldn't see." Telford, p. 5.

p. 13   "We'd been carting...all the air." Blassingame, p. 461.

p. 13   "I seemed to see...couldn't reach them." Humez, p. 214.

Chapter Three

p. 17   "Every time...carried away." Humez, p. 279.

p. 17   "a happy...harmless one." Martin, p. 360.

p. 19   Among other 1832 state laws restricting the rights of African Americans was an Alabama law that set a fine of up to five hundred dollars for teaching any *free* black to read. Also, any free black who associated with slaves without the permission of their owners was subject to a whipping. According to an 1832 Virginia law, any class meeting to teach African Americans was an "unlawful assembly." People at such a meeting were to be whipped. (Bergman, pp. 142–45.)

p. 19-20 "Appears like...ready for me." Telford, p. 6.

p. 21 "She was very...splendid memory." Humez, p. 210.

p. 22 "Every time...carried away." Lowry, p. 117.

p. 22 "O, dear Lord...a Christian." Bradford, p. 14.

p. 22 "If you ain't...no more mischief." Clinton, p. 31.

p. 22 "He died just...a bad, wicked man." Lowry, p. 127.

p. 22-23 "I'd give...for him no longer." Larson, p. 73.

p. 23 "I was always...all my sins." Bradford, p. 14.

p. 23 "They're coming...I must go." Lowry, p. 130.

p. 24 "Go along...milking tonight." Humez, p. 215.

p. 25 "*I'm sorry, friends...the promised land.*" Bradford, p. 16.

p. 25 "I had reasoned...take me." Ibid, p. 17.

Chapter Four

p. 26 "I felt . . . in heaven." Larson, p. 84

p. 28 "must have...underground road." Gara, p. 174.

p. 28 "I looked at...in heaven." Bradford, pp. 17–18.

p. 28-29 "He was always...land of freedom." Bradford, p. 18.

p. 29 "MINTY aged about...in the State."

p. 29-30 In 1850 there were 10,736 free blacks in Philadelphia, 2,176 of them were in school. Of the 25,442 free blacks in Baltimore, the most in any city in the country, only 1,453 were in school. The information on free blacks and schools in Philadelphia is from Bergman, pp. 189–95. Larson, p. 79.

p. 30 "I was free...my help." Bradford, p. 18.

Chapter Five

p. 33 "Joe, you're...a free man!" Bradford, p. 28.

p. 34 "Who's there?"..."William Penn."

p. 34 "By tomorrow...no back charges." *New York Times*, June 4, 1899, p. IM12.

p. 36 "If our...be cowards," Bacon, p. 57.

p. 36 "Gentlemen...sing for you." Humez, p. 237.

p. 37 "Thee hasn't...*Thomas Garrett.*" Katz, p. 167.

p. 38-39 "She had faithfully...before or since." Still, pp. 296–97.

p. 39 "Moses has got...the power." Humez, p. 259.

p. 39 "Didn't you almost...one bit." Ibid, p. 259.

p. 39-40 "It wasn't me...always did." Ibid, p. 261.

p. 40 "Suppose I...your brother?" Bordewich, p. 357.

p. 41 "talked like...to the ground." Still, p. 73.

p. 41 "promoted from the U.G.R.R." Ibid, p. 51.

Chapter Six

p. 42 "I wouldn't trust...to Canada." Bradford, p. 22.

p. 44 "I had never...filthy enactment." Benton, V. 8, pp. 261–262.

p. 45 "It is an act of insurrection." Still, p. 353.

p. 45 "a foul stain...our state." Ibid, p. 354.

p. 48 "Underground Rail Road stock...to the other." Ibid, p. 368.

p. 50-51 "How foolish...make mischief...If he could...without him...dropped out." Humez, p. 219.

Chapter Seven

p. 52 "I've served my...the lash, abroad." Bradford, p. 27.

p. 52-53 "On one occasion...barn loft." Douglass, p. 254.

p. 53 "Hail, oh hail...let me go." Lowry, pp. 180–181.

p. 53 "Tell my brothers...step aboard." Bradford, p. 34.

p. 55 "Harriet and one...fit them out." Still, p. 296.

p. 55 "Shout...are free!" Lowry, p. 194.

p. 57 "A wolf...pretending to preach for twenty years." Still, p. 396.

p. 57 "They seemed delighted...getting to Canada." Still, p. 396.

p. 58 "Who are you?...on a nail." Bradford, pp. 30–31.

p. 58 "I'm going to...see me through." Bradford, p. 33.

p. 58 "Children...cross the river." Ibid, p. 39.

p. 58 "The water never...the other side." Ibid, p. 40.

p. 59 "It wasn't me. It was the Lord!" Ibid, p. 33. The text in Bradford is: "'twan't me, 'twas de Lord!")

Chapter Eight

p. 60 "When I think...God in him." Humez, p. 243.

p. 60 "possesses...shrewdness." Ibid, p. 30.

p. 60 "He was a...a soldier." Benton, V.9, p. 137.

p. 62 "Come with me...hive them." Douglass, p. 309.

p. 62 "My discretion...about their criticisms." Ibid, pp. 309–10.

p. 63 "I knew he was coming." Lowry, p. 234.

p. 63 "wilderness sort of...long white beard." Clinton, p. 124.

p. 65 "I had...no husband." Larson, p. 167.

p. 66 "a handsome sum...Mr. Seward." Bradford, p. 61.

p. 66 "They can't...pull us up." Humez, p. 38.

p. 66 "one of the...this continent." Larson, p. 166.

p. 67 "He needed...not exist." Benton, V. 9, p 140.

p. 67 "I...make insurrection." Ibid, V. 9, pp 143 – 44.

p. 67 "would willingly...cause of freedom." *Vincennes Gazette*, an Indiana newspaper, November 19, 1859.

p. 67 "Be of good...all things well." *John Brown's letters to his wife, Mary Day Brown, from the prison at Charlestown*, http://www.law.umkc .edu/faculty/projects/ftrials/johnbrown/ brownprisonletters.html

p. 67-68 "quite certain...but with blood." Martin, p. 435.

p. 68 "For a year...by the mob." Still, p. 531.

p. 68 "She had often...not understand." Bradford, pp. 61–62.

p. 68 "He done more...in living." Humez, p. 308.

Chapter Nine

p. 71 "Go it...ever had." Humez, p. 239.

p. 72 "Here they come...Take him!" Lowry, p. 263

p. 72 "Give us liberty...us death." Larson, p. 181.

p. 72 "Drag him to...them have him!" Ibid, p. 182.

p. 74 "I write to...I have hope." Still, pp. 530–531.

Chapter Ten

p. 75 "They say...about the Negro." Humez, p. 249.

p. 75 "We are two...is inevitable." Martin, p. 430.

p. 77 "Apprehension seems...but friends." Lossing, v. 5, p. 425

p. 77 "They may say...going to be war!" Conrad, p. 33.

p. 78 "Having defended...General Beauregard." McMaster, p. 195

p. 82-83 "My people are...cease this noise...are free." Telford, p. 15.

p. 83 "Secretly and...northern home." Humez, p. 269.

p. 83 "Neither she...ever been slaves." Ibid, p. 269.

p. 84   "Mother looked…Aunt Harriet." Ibid, p. 270.

p. 84   "to speak…as a lady." Humez, p. 270.

p. 84   "Never wound…kill it." Conrad, p. 35.

p. 86   "I intend…claims to be." Botkin, p. 53

p. 86   "They changed…program." Telford, p. 15.

Chapter Eleven

p. 87   "The good Lord…help him." Humez, p. 249.

p. 87   "They wouldn't…he came down." Larson, p. 204.

p. 90   "Most of them…their own living." Conrad, pp. 36–37.

p. 90   "ready to go." Bradford, p. 52.

p. 90-91 "It is the masters…loyal soldiers…fugitive rebels." *New York Times*, May 3, 1896, p. 26.

p. 91   "Mr. Lincoln took…That will do." Botkin, pp. 233–234.

p. 91   "enraged tyrant." Adams, p. 282.

p. 92   "God Almighty's…land of freedom!" Kirshon, p. 375.

p. 92   "I had my…no more." Telford, p. 15.

p. 93   "I never seen…Jeff Davis." Botkin, p. 150.

p. 93   "Moses…a song." Ibid, p. 151.

p. 95   "*Come from…all a farm.*" Humez, p. 246.

Chapter Twelve

p. 96   "And now a word…vaunt their patriotism." Humez, p. 300.

p. 96   "We saw the lightening…that we reaped." Larson, p. 220.

p. 96   "Men lying…unnatural shapes." Clinton, p. 178.

p. 98   "I would go…thick as ever." Telford, p. 17.

p. 98   "I only did my duty." www.united-states-flag.com/fort-wagner.html.

p. 99   There is no telling…and their families." *New York Times*, May 3, 1896, p. 26.

p. 99   "They are far…tortured and hung…desperate fighters." Bergman, pp. 232–233.

p. 99-100 "They was dying…it cured them." Telford, p.16.

p. 100   "I didn't like…like that." Lowry, p. 345.

p. 101   "Richmond must be evacuated this evening." Elson, p. 770.

p. 101   "From that moment…pandemonium reigned." *The New York Times*, April 8, 1865, p. 1.

p. 102   "father or master Abraham…had gone crazy." *The Christian Recorder*, April 22, 1865.

p. 104   "of course…state of Ohio…of the righteous." Ibid, April 22, 1865.

p. 104-105 "We fought…to say more." Muzzey, p. 466.

p. 105   "The war is over…gallant foe." Evans, p. 395.

p. 105   "How many thousands…beloved fathers!" *The Christian Recorder*, April 29, 1865.

Chapter Thirteen

p. 107   "You wouldn't think…under its folds." Humez, p. 254.

p. 108-109 "The night was…Intense grief…than of whites." Benton, v. 9, pp. 576–577.

p. 109   "dreadful abuses" Larson, p. 229.

p. 110   "Come, hustle out of here!" Larson, p. 232.

p. 110   "copperhead scoundrel." Larson, p. 232.

p. 110   "proud of…of being white." Lowry, p. 349.

p. 111   "Put on the…the big one." Lowry, p. 350.

Chapter Fourteen

p. 116   "I am at…all mankind." Humez, p. 257.

p. 116   "Just before the…glided out again." Clinton, p. 200.

p. 120   "I read your book…you this medal…She also invited…enough to go." Humez, p. 255. "a state of terror…of the people." Van Doren, p. 249. "Now I die happy." Larson, p. 276.

p. 121   "If those deeds…what do?" Humez, p. 315.

p. 121   "a faithful worker…of her race." Ibid, p. 319.

p. 121-122 "The old woman…dignity of her appearance…noble assistance." Ibid, pp. 319–320.

p. 122   "Yes, ladies…never lost a passenger." Ibid, p. 253.

p. 122   "When I was…Sir, do you…more comfortable." Larson, p. 282.

p. 123   "for a woman...and her wit keen."
Larson, p. 287.

p. 123   "We drove into...Well & brisk." Humez,
pp. 329–330.

p. 123   "I go to prepare a place for you." Clinton,
p. 214.

p. 125   "She joined...ready to die." Humez, pp.
328–329.

p. 125   "as resolute...Her sound mind...of her
race...for many years." Ibid, p. 331.

p. 125-126   "Something like this could never...charity
for all." Ibid, pp. 331–332.

p. 126   "This tablet will...and unselfish." Ibid,
p. 336.

p. 126   "We have met...heroic soul." Ibid, p. 334.

p. 127   "One of the greatest of . . . all time."
Conrad, p. 47.

Author's Note

The sources of my family's Civil War
history are my father Sidney G. Adler and
Gottesman, pp. 13–20.

SELECTED BIBLIOGRAPHY

Adams, James Truslow. *America's Tragedy.* New York:
Scribner, 1934.

Allen, Thomas B. *Harriet Tubman: Secret Agent.*
Washington, DC: National Geographic, 2006.

Andrews, E. Benjamin. *History of the United States,* Vol.
III. New York: Scribner, 1895.

Bacon, Margaret Hope. *Valiant Friend: The Life of Lucretia
Mott.* New York: Walker, 1980.

Benton, William, ed. *The Annals of America.* Chicago:
Encyclopedia Britannica, 1968.

Bergman, Peter M. *The Chronological History of the Negro
in America.* New York: Harper, 1969.

Blassingame, John H., ed. *Slave Testimony.* Baton Rouge:
Louisiana State University, 1977.

Blight, David W. *Passages to Freedom.* Washington, DC:
Smithsonian, 2004.

Blockson, Charles L. *The Underground Railroad.* New
York: Prentice Hall, 1987.

Bordewich, Fergus M. *Bound for Canaan: The
Underground Railroad and the War for the Soul of
America.* New York: Amistad/Harper, 2005.

Botkin, B. A. *A Civil War Treasury of Tales Legends and
Folklore.* New York: Random House, 1960.

Bradford, Sarah H. *Harriet Tubman: The Moses of Her
People.* Mineola, NY: Dover, 2004.

Bright, Col. Marshal H. *True Stories of American History.*
Philadelphia: John C. Winston, 1898.

Clinton, Catherine. *Harriet Tubman.* Boston: Little
Brown, 2004.

Conrad, Earl. *Harriet Tubman: Negro Soldier and
Abolitionist.* New York: International, 1942.

Donnelly, T. F. *A Primary History of the United States.* New
York: American Book, 1919.

Douglass, Frederick. *The Life and Times of Frederick
Douglass: An Autobiography.* New York: Gramercy,
1993.

Elson, Henry William. *History of the United States of
America.* New York: MacMillan, 1922.

Eusebius, Mary. "A Modern Moses: Harriet Tubman."
The Journal of Negro Education, Vol. 19, No. 1,
Winter 1950, pp. 16–27.

Evans, Lawton B. *America First: One Hundred Stories from
Our History.* Springfield, MA: Milton Bradley,
1920.

Gara, Larry. *The Liberty Line: The Legend of the
Underground Railroad.* Lexington: University
Press of Kentucky, 1996.

Garraty, John A, and Jerome L. Sternstein. *Encyclopedia of
American Biography.* New York: HarperCollins, 1996.

Gorrell, Gena K. *North Star to Freedom: The Story of the
Underground Railroad.* New York: Delacorte, 1997.

Gottesman, Milton M. *Hoopskirts and Huppas: A Chronicle
of the Early Years of the Garfunkel-Trager Family in
America.* New York: American Jewish Historical
Society, 1999.

Grant, Callie Smith. *Harriet Tubman.* Uhrichsville, OH:
Barbour, 2002.

Hawthorne, Julian. *The History of the United States,*
Volumes I, II, and III. New York: Collier, 1912.

Humez, Jean M. *Harriet Tubman: The Life and Stories.*
Madison: University of Wisconsin Press, 2003.

Katz, William Loren. *Eyewitness: A Living Documentary of the
African American Contribution to American History.*
New York: Touchstone, Simon and Schuster, 1995.

Keylin, Arleen, and Douglas John Bowen, eds. *New York
Times: Book of the Civil War.* New York: Arno
Press, 1980.

Kirshon, John W., editor-in-chief. *Chronicle of America.*
Mount Kisco, NY: Chronicle, 1989.

Larson, Kate Clifford. *Bound for the Promised Land: Harriet Tubman, Portrait of an American Hero*. New York: Ballantine, 2004.

Lossing, Benson John. *Harper's Encyclopedia of United States History*, 10 volumes. New York: Harper, 1907.

Lowry, Beverly. *Harriet Tubman: Imagining a Life*. New York: Doubleday, 2007.

Martin, James Kirby, Randy Roberts, Steven Mintz, Linda O. McMurry, and James H. Jones. *America and Its People*. New York: Harper, 1989.

Muzzey, David Saville. *An American History*. Boston: Ginn, 1917.

Ridpath, John Clark. *Ridpath's History of the United States*. Philadelphia: Historical Publishing, 1897.

Sernett, Milton C. *Harriet Tubman: Myth, Memory, and History*. Durham, NC: Duke University Press, 2007.

Sterling, Dorothy, ed. *We Are Your Sisters*. New York: Norton, 1984.

Still, William. *The Underground Railroad: A Record*. Philadelphia: Porter and Coates, 1872.

Taylor, M. W. *Harriet Tubman: Antislavery Activist*. New York: Chelsea, 1991.

Telford, Emma P. *Harriet: The Modern Moses of Heroism and Visions*. Aurora, NY: Cayuga Museum, 1905.

Tobin, Jacqueline L, and Raymond G. Dobard. *Hidden in Plain View: The Secret Story of Quilts and the Underground Railroad*. New York: Doubleday, 1999.

Van Doren, Charles. *The Negro in American History*, Vol. I Encyclopedia Britannica Educational Corporation, 1969.

Wheeler, Richard. *Sherman's March*. New York: Crowell, 1978.

http://www.law.umkc.edu/faculty/projects/ftrials/johnbrown/brownprisonletters.html

PICTURE CREDITS:

Andrews, E. Benjamin. *History of the United States*, Vol. III. New York: Scribner, 1895: pages 18, 64, 94

Barnard, George N. *Photographic Views of Sherman's March*. Mineola, NY: Dover, 1977: page 130

Barlett, *W.H. Barlett's Classic Illustrations of America*. Mincola: Dover, 1977: pages 50, 63, 70

Bright, Col. Marshal H. *True Stories of American History*. Philadelphia: John C. Winston, 1898: pages 8, 20

Cirker, Howard and Blanche, ed. *Pictionary of American Portraits*, New York: Dover, 1917: pages 73, 74, 98(top)

Civil War Illustrations: Electronic Clip Art. Mineola, NY: Dover, 2003: pages 77, 78(both), 79,80, 82, 85, 91(top), 92, 97, 101, 102, 104(both), 105, 107, 108, 119

Famous Americans: Electronic Clip Art. Mineola, NY: Dover, 2005: pages 35, 36(top), 44, 49, 76, 91(bottom), 98(bottom)

Faris, John T. *Real Stories from Our History*. Boston: Ginn, 1916: page 30

James, James Alton, and Albert Hart Sanford. *American History*. New York: Scribner, 1913: page 56 (bottom)

Lawlor, Thomas Bonaventure, *A Primary History of teh United States*. Boston: Ginn, 1905: page 16

Lossing, Benson John. *Harper's Encyclopedia of United States History*, 10 volumes. New York: Harper, 1907: page 6, 118 (top)

McMaster, John Bach. *A Primary History of the United States*. New York: American Book, 1901: page 17, 87

Muzzey, David Saville. *An American History*. Boston: Ginn, 1917: page 118(bottom)

New York Public Library, Photographs and Print Division Shomburg Center for Research in Black Culture, Aster Lenox and Tilden Foundations: pages iv, 39, 83, 124, 129

Ridpath, John Clark. *Ridpath's History of the United States*. Philadelphia: Historical Publishing, 1897: pages 43, 38

Still, William. *The Underground Railroad: A Record*. Philadelphia: Porter and Coates, 1872: pages 4, 24, 27, 28, 31, 34, 36(bottom), 38, 40, 45, 55, 56(top)

INDEX

Page numbers in *italics* refer to illustrations.